Praise for *The*

In this devotional, you will find strength for your struggle, comfort in the challenge, hope for the hard times, and beauty in the mess. Each chapter is written from the heart of my generous and wise friends. In giving away their lives and story, Debbie and Elaine provide a God-breathed guide for your own journey. I'm so grateful for the love and example that is tangible on each page. I know it is going to bless many.

Charlotte Gambill
International Speaker and Author

I love Debbie and Elaine. I've known them since I was a child, and I've seen their love for God and their love for others. This book is such a beautiful expression of who they are, with stories and truths that are as relatable as they are profound. You'll discover there isn't a mess God can't handle, and there isn't a moment He can't bring about something good. No matter what season of life you're in, this book will encourage you just as it has encouraged me. Debbie and Elaine, thank you for writing this!

Kari Jobe Carnes
Worship Leader

In the field of mother-daughter duos who are also vocational ministry leaders, Debbie and Elaine are world champions! They navigate the pits and pinnacles of life with palpable faith in the sufficient grace of God and the fact that they're willing to share what they've learned along the way with such authenticity and sound biblical guidance is a gift for the rest of us! This devotional will be on Missy's and my nightstand for a long time.

Lisa Harper
Bible Teacher, Speaker, Author of LIFE

THE GOOD MESS

Finding Beauty in
Imperfect Moments

THE GOOD MESS

Finding Beauty in Imperfect Moments

DEBBIE MORRIS
ELAINE FISHER

TABLE OF CONTENTS

To Elaine—I am so proud of the woman you have become,
and I love the relationship we have.
You know I was hesitant about writing this devotional,
but you can talk me into anything!
And I'm so glad you did.

To Mom, my best friend—I am so honored to have this friendship,
and my heart is to always steward it well.
What a gift to write this book together!
You are my hero, and I want to be like you when I grow up.

INTRODUCTION

There's a story in the Bible we are drawn to, but it may not be for the reasons you think. It's a story about a woman named Hannah. When we first meet her, she's desperate and distraught and crying out to God for a baby.

You see, in her time children represented significance, value, importance, legacy, and stability. It was a social, financial, and familial expectation. Yet Hannah did not have any children.

Hannah goes to the temple to pray, and her prayers are full of anguish. She's moaning and crying. Quite honestly, she's a *mess*. So much so that the priest Eli thinks she's drunk! But while she's there, she has a miraculous encounter with the Lord. She knows God heard her prayers, and she leaves a changed woman.

First Samuel 1:18 then says, "So [Hannah] went her way and ate, and her face was no longer sad." Other Bible versions use the word "countenance" here instead of face. The Message translation goes as far to say, "Then she ate heartily, her face radiant." Hannah's face changed, her attitude changed, her appetite changed. Everything about her changed. But why? She didn't leave the temple pregnant. She didn't even leave the temple with a concrete answer to her prayer. Her external circumstances weren't altered one bit.

Hannah changed because she had an *encounter* with the Lord in the middle of her mess. The miracle she had been praying for hadn't happened yet, but another miracle occurred. Hannah was lifted out of her despair. She walked away knowing she was seen, cared for, and known by an almighty God who heard her prayers. Hannah's encounter with the Lord gave her courage and strength to face the days to come.

People tend to focus on the second part of this story, about the miracle child Hannah conceives—Samuel. And yes, he *is* a miracle! But that miracle may not have happened if the first miracle had not happened—an *encounter* with God! The reason the first miracle happened is because Hannah turned to God in her despair. She didn't allow her despair or frustration to keep her from the temple and ultimately, God. Instead, she brought everything, her whole self, mess and all, to the Lord.

At one time or another, we've all had something we're pursuing the Lord for and asking Him to do for us. Life is tough. Some days it's messy. We've all cried out, "God, I need You to show up. I need You to do something about this situation!" Maybe you're a new wife, and you're trying to find a

> God knows you, He sees you, He has great plans for you, He loves you, and He is with you always—even in the messes of life.

new rhythm to your days. Perhaps you're a mom with multiple kids, and you're just trying to find time to shower. Maybe you're lonely and having trouble finding godly friends. Maybe you're an empty nester, and while you've looked forward to this moment, now that it's here, you're not sure what to do with yourself. Or maybe you're taking care of an aging parent or a sick spouse right now, and life is just difficult. Whatever it is, God sees you. And we know that no matter what you're worried about, what clutter you're trying to muddle through, or what you're carrying, at the end of the day, what you really need is an encounter with a gracious and loving God.

Our guess is, in picking up this book, you are at least open to bringing your mess to the Lord. And what we know from personal experience is that He wants an encounter with you. Which is why we wrote this book. We want to take a journey with you for the next thirty-six days and focus on encountering the Lord in the middle of those less-than-perfect moments of life. We have learned this can and will change *everything*.

Within these pages, we're going to tell stories about our family and our lives. We'll share our mistakes and our victories as moms, wives, daughters, leaders, and friends. Neither of us are perfect, but God has done beautiful things out of our best, worst, and sometimes misguided intentions. We'll talk a lot about expectations and seasons and being present. We'll challenge you some days and encourage you in others. You'll hear the perspective of two different generations—mom and daughter who have become best friends. We'll keep things short because we know life is busy. And we hope you'll take a deep breath, laugh with us, and learn from our experiences, however messy they are.

But overall, throughout this devotional, we pray you have God-breathed encounters that change how you look at life. We hope you begin to see that every mess is an opportunity for God to do something beautiful. We pray for you to experience supernatural courage and strength in the days to come, whatever struggles, pain, monotony, chaos, or confusion you may face. We don't have all the answers, but we know the One who does! Our prayer is for God to show up and be personal with you. For Him to change your face—no Botox needed!

We believe the miraculous answered prayers will come too, but what we really want for you to experience within every story and every word written here is the knowledge that God knows you, He sees you, He has great plans for you, He loves you, and He is with you always—even in the messes of life.

Hannah's hot mess breakdown at the temple turned into a good thing. Because of her encounter, she was able to wipe the mascara off her face and walk away with hope. We pray that you walk away from this devotional with a "radiant face" and ready to "eat heartily" because you had a life-changing encounter with our almighty God.

Debbie + Elaine

LET'S EAT!

Debbie Morris

Rejoice always, pray without ceasing, in everything give thanks;
for this is the will of God in Christ Jesus for you.

1 Thessalonians 5:16–18

One day when I was growing up, my mom, my sister, and I spent the whole day cleaning the house for guests who were coming over for dinner. I can't remember who was coming to see us, but they must have been important because we cleaned *all day*. As a crowning touch to the dinner she was making, my mom also made a pie. It had a graham cracker crust with bananas, a cream cheese filling, and berries on top. She was getting ready to put the special dessert in the refrigerator to chill, but as she lifted it up off the counter, the pie toppled and went splat on the floor we had just mopped!

I'll never forget how we all just stood there looking at the mess. Then my mom reached into the silverware drawer, took out three spoons, and with a grin said, "Let's eat!" We sat on the floor together and ate as much pie as we wanted. When our bellies were full, we cleaned it up and went about the rest of our day.

This is such a sweet memory to me. It wasn't just about eating the delicious pie; it was how my mom didn't let an accident ruin our whole day. In the same way that pie covered our floor, my mom covered that situation with grace and a good attitude. It was truly a gift.

I thought about that moment recently when I was making lamb chops for my husband, Robert. I decided to use a new bacon barbeque sauce that someone had given us as a gift. The bottle looked kind of fancy and had an old-fashioned soda drink top, and as I began to open it, the sauce started spilling out. I put the bottle in the sink and continued to let off a little bit of pressure on the top when it suddenly exploded! Barbeque sauce with little bacon bits went *everywhere*! It coated my hair, my clothes, the counters, the backsplash, *and* the *ceiling*! You could even see a Debbie-shaped sauce outline on the wall behind me.

I blinked in shock and then just started laughing. It was so bad and such a mess that I was beyond tears—I could only laugh!

> **The good things
> in life are
> often messy.**

Robert heard the commotion and came into the kitchen and asked, "What are you laughing about?" and I responded, "This!" with a huge smile and my arms open wide. He took a picture of my predicament, and we laughed some more as I cleaned it up. (You might even remember seeing us post a video about this on social media!) To this day, if you look closely, you can still see sauce stains on our walls!

Life is full of mistakes and accidents and messes. It's inevitable. At some point, something is going to go splat all over the floor—or the walls! And sometimes it's going to stain. Proverbs 14:4 (NLT) says, "Without oxen a stable stays clean, but you need a strong ox for a large harvest." The good things in life are often messy. You can't have a clean stable *and* a large harvest.

But how many times have we flipped our lid because something got messed up or didn't go the way we planned? How many times have we "cried over spilled milk"? Maybe you had an instant negative reaction, and then afterward, you sat back and thought, *Why did I lose it like that?* These curveball moments don't have to ruin us—whether it's a mistake at work or a sticky mess the kids made. When we expect the inevitability of the messes of life and count them as byproducts of blessing, we can embrace these moments, and depending on what they are, even find joy in them.

You might not be able to change the situation, but you can change how you react to it. Life is too short to spend your days cranky about things that go wrong. Close your eyes. Take a deep breath. And ask the Lord to fill you with His peace.

With the Holy Spirit's leading, you can respond differently than your flesh may desire. You can react to life's messes with joy, gratitude, forgiveness, grace, peace—and even laughter! You can *choose* the attitude with which you approach your days, and that might change everything for yourself and the people around you.

How do we do that? I believe the more time we spend with Jesus and learn His ways, the more the Holy Spirit will empower us to be like Him, in the small messes and the big. With His help, we can approach our messes with gratitude and grace.

So grab a spoon, there's a mess to enjoy!

Finding Beauty in the Mess

What messes can you rejoice in today?
Take a moment with the Lord right now, and ask Him
to give you joy, gratitude, and grace throughout your day.

DAY 2

CHOOSING TO BE PRESENT

Debbie Morris

But Martha was distracted with much serving, and she approached Him and said, "Lord, do You not care that my sister has left me to serve alone? Therefore tell her to help me." And Jesus answered and said to her, "Martha, Martha, you are worried and troubled about many things. But one thing is needed, and Mary has chosen that good part, which will not be taken away from her."

Luke 10:40–42

One Christmas when our kids were younger, after weeks of preparing, cleaning, shopping, fretting, wrapping, and organizing—it hit me! Out of nowhere—*it hit me!* A snowball made of tinsel, tissue, and wrapping paper smacked me in the head. Not some metaphorical thought, but a real-life paper snowball. The atomic paper wasn't intended for me, but I got hit in the crossfire. You see, when our kids, along with their cousins, realized they were too old to be grounded, they started something I am confident is unique to our family. Every neatly wrapped present is a potential weapon. As each gift is unwrapped, the paper is wadded up into a ball. The kids try to wait until all the gifts are opened, but self-restraint doesn't run deep when the opportunity presents itself to smack an inattentive relative in the face with a paper snowball.

None of us sit around the table remembering what we had for dinner or how the tree was decorated last year, but the kids still debate who drew "first blood" years ago and who got in the best shot in this year's wrapping paper snowball fight. It's not a tradition we envisioned for our family, but I couldn't have planned it better!

We still wrap gifts, decorate the tree, and try to cook a delicious meal because we love our families and want things to be special. We look forward to the glimmer in the eyes of our grandkids as they discover the wonder of the holidays. But I have learned to relax and be present because the best moments are likely to just hit me in the head.

I like to think I learned this from Mary and Martha. Martha thought she was choosing to do the most important things—cooking, cleaning, and hosting—but these only distracted her from enjoying time with her family and their special

> **Every day with those we love is a precious gift.**

guest, Jesus. She was missing precious time with the King of kings and Lord of lords because she was "distracted with much serving." Then there was Mary, who chose to be present over busyness. Scripture calls her choice the "good part."

How many times have we chosen to be busy instead of spending time with loved ones? How many times do we miss moments with our family because we're too worried about having a clean kitchen? Yes, the dishes need to be done, but they can wait a little longer. Years from now, you won't remember your clean house or the table centerpiece that took three trips to the store to find. But you'll remember the song your son made up about the glories of chocolate pie, how your niece fell asleep with her head on your shoulder, or how a ball of wrapping paper hit you in the face.

While preparations are good and often necessary, especially around the holidays, there's a time and place for them, and may I say, it's not when everyone is together. I would like to encourage you to relax from your to-do list and be mindful of the moments you have with your kids or grandkids. Every day with those we love is a precious gift, and as they grow, you will greatly miss the little hugs, elated screams, silly conversations, and sleepy smiles of days past.

What will it take for you to be present and enjoy time with your family? Because being together, making memories, telling funny stories, having "snowball fights" . . . *those* are the really good parts of life. And sometimes the best memories are created when you're not looking for them.

So, *duck! Incoming!* Wrapping paper snowballs are headed your way (metaphorically, of course!).

Finding Beauty in the Mess

Being present takes intentionality.
Will you choose to be present during family times?
What steps do you need to take to make this happen?

EMBRACE THE DIFFERENCES

Debbie Morris

My soul, wait silently for God alone,
for my expectation is from Him.

Psalm 62:5

Elaine is the little girl I always wanted. I mean, I love my boys (this is where Elaine would jump in and say, "Nope, the boys were just distractions until I got here!"), but Robert and I *really* wanted a girl too.

After I had Josh and James, I tried getting pregnant again, but it didn't happen as quickly as I expected. A few years in, I started thinking that two boys were probably all we were going to have, and I was grateful! But Robert would never let go of the belief that we were going to have a baby girl. He challenged me to have faith and really believe with him for a daughter. I didn't want to get hurt in believing for something that wouldn't happen, so this was a stretch for me, a hesitant leap. But I chose to have faith and believe that God would honor our heart's desire.

When I finally got pregnant five years later, we were ecstatic! And we *knew* the baby was a girl. We didn't need a sonogram to find out! Elaine was the gift we desperately wanted that I hesitantly dared to ask for.

One night, when I was feeding her, the Lord dropped in my heart that she was not going to be a carbon copy of me, and I needed to be prepared. I had initially thought Elaine was going to be just like me and have some of my best traits—easygoing and quiet and gentle. But I had a sense from the Lord that this was not going to be the case.

And sure enough, Elaine challenged *all* my thinking right from the start! I even lost the clothing battle when she was only six months old. I would put something on her, and she would throw a fit until I changed her outfit. At the time I thought, *Oh, those clothes must irritate her.* But the truth was she had an opinion, and she didn't like the clothes I had chosen for her that day.

Over the years, I had to realize again and again that she's *not* me. I couldn't expect her to be. For instance, she has a very strong, loud voice. And as she was growing up, I would

> **Jesus is more than we can imagine or expect.**

start to tell her to speak quietly, but then I'd think, *No, I'm not going to tell her to be quiet. She's different than me.* (Elaine always says, "Quiet is not in my vocabulary.") I really tried not to put her in a box or expect her to be anything but who God made her to be. I see Elaine now, as a pastor and brilliant communicator, and I wonder what would've happened if I had tried to limit her or force her to be more like me.

Now, more than ever, I appreciate and love that she's totally different than me. I see so much of her dad in her, although she's not entirely him either. And I believe my acceptance that she's her own person has actually helped foster the close relationship we have now. But if the Lord had not prepared my heart for this when she was young, I might not have embraced the differences between us. And I think this "embracing" has been the key to our deep friendship as she's grown into an adult. (Oh, to think what we might have missed!)

The Bible gives us a great example of when people formed an incorrect expectation about someone: when Jesus came to earth in human form. There were plenty of years of waiting before He arrived, and yet people still dared to believe He would show up. But then, when He did, He crushed all expectations. He came as a vulnerable baby, in a small town full of lowly shepherds. Jesus grew up to be nothing like the conquering King the people expected Him to be. He didn't overthrow Rome. He didn't sit on an earthly throne. He taught humility and generosity and love above all, even above one's own life. Then He died a criminal's death. When we throw out our misguided expectations of who we want Him to be, we can see Him for who He truly is. Jesus is *more* than we can imagine or expect. When we finally realize this, we open ourselves to a close, raw, and exciting relationship with Him, and we can live our lives with peace instead of disappointment or frustration.

I don't know what expectations you have for your life or relationships. Maybe, like me, you expected a quiet, easygoing daughter and got a loud, stubborn one. Maybe you expected to be married by now, but instead you're on your own. Or maybe you expected to be in a much more successful place in your career, but you're still in that small cubicle on the third floor.

Take some time today to think about any expectations you have put on yourself, your relationships, and your future. Remember, though, that not all expectations are bad. We can expect God's eternal love, Jesus' second return, and the sun to rise each morning. But when expectations are unfair, unreasonable, or unrealistic, they can hinder us from experiencing true joy in every day.

Place your hope and expectation in God alone. You might be surprised by what He has in store for you.

Finding Beauty in the Mess

Bring your expectations to the Lord today.
Ask Him to give you a vision of how He sees your
circumstances, your relationships, and your future.

JUST ONE LITTLE LIE

Elaine Fisher

Now the serpent was more cunning than any beast of the field which the LORD God had made. And he said to the woman, "Has God indeed said, 'You shall not eat of every tree of the garden'?"

Genesis 3:1

When I was in middle school, a boy asked me to be his girlfriend. I was so excited and went home to ask my dad if it was okay. With a bit of a laugh, he said, "Elaine, you're in fifth grade, and neither of you have jobs or can drive to go on a date by yourselves. So what does this mean?" He made some valid points, so I went to school the next day and told the boy my dad said I couldn't be his girlfriend.

But his best friend was listening close by and said to me, "Elaine, how will your dad ever know?" My dad was busy with starting Gateway Church at the time, so I thought about it and said, "Well, I guess he wouldn't!" So I said "Yes!" to this boy and became his girlfriend.

And you know what happened? Nothing. Or so I thought.

The truth is a seed was planted and got me thinking about how my dad said I couldn't date that boy to protect my heart, but then, when I chose to do it anyway, nothing bad happened. Did my dad not want me to have fun? Was he being overly protective or selfish? And then another little question entered my brain: *does my dad really have my best interests at heart?*

What seemed like an innocent situation became a wedge that threatened my relationship with my dad and indirectly, with the Lord. With much thought and prodding from the enemy, the seed that was planted took root, and that question soon turned into a statement: *my dad may not have my best interests at heart.*

I began to doubt a lot of things, specifically the nature of my dad's love for me. In the hustle and bustle of ministry life, I don't think anyone realized that my heart had started to harden toward the church, toward my parents, and toward God.

Years later when I started dating an older guy, my parents told

> So many times,
> the enemy will add or
> take away a word or two
> from what God says in
> order to deceive us.

me he was dangerous and I needed to stop seeing him, but once again that little lie popped up into my mind, and I chose to believe it. I didn't listen to my parents' warnings, and I continued to date this guy behind their backs, even after getting caught a couple of times. That's when things really went downhill.

There's someone else I often think about who believed a lie and then things went majorly downhill: Eve. You know the story. The Lord warned her and Adam not to eat the fruit of only one specific tree in a huge garden of trees. It really wasn't an unreasonable request. Then the enemy showed up and cast doubt on the Lord's words, "'Has God indeed said, 'You shall not eat of every tree of the garden'?'" (Genesis 3:1). Eve then responded with the words God commanded about that one specific tree, "'You shall not eat it, nor shall you touch it, lest you die.' Then the serpent said to the woman, 'You will not surely die. For God knows that in the day you eat of it your eyes will be opened, and you will be like God, knowing good and evil'" (vv. 3–5). So many times, the enemy will add or take away a word or two from what God says in order to deceive us. He did that here to entice Eve to question God's provision, protection, and love—to question whether her Father was holding out on her or had her best interests at heart. Sounds familiar, doesn't it? The enemy isn't creative. He uses the same tactics again and again.

When the wrong voices become the trusted voices in your life, it can derail your journey. I can tell you from personal experience that one lie, no matter how big or small, can lead to a hardening of your heart toward the truth and impaired decision-making. And in the case of Eve, the fall of all mankind into sin.

So how do we protect ourselves from questions and thoughts that cast doubt on the truth? We turn to the Word of God. Romans 12:2 says that we must renew our minds, and 2 Corinthians 10:5 says to take our thoughts captive. We must be vigilant to take captive *every* thought that comes into our minds. Scripture is our God-empowered weapon of warfare. And no lie or falsehood can stand when we focus on the truth of God's Word.

Finding Beauty in the Mess

What lies are you believing about yourself, your loved ones, or God? Take time today to examine your thoughts, and lasso any that do not line up with the truth of God's Word. Ask the Holy Spirit to guide you and fill your heart and mind with His truth today.

BRINGING IT TO LIGHT

Elaine Fisher

*Confess your sins to each other and
pray for each other so that you may be healed.
The earnest prayer of a righteous person has great power and
produces wonderful results.*

James 5:16 (NLT)

I was in so deep, I didn't know how to get out. As a teenager, I went to church for the free snacks and the attention of being a pastor's kid, but the rest of my life was filled with partying, abuse, sexual sin, and anger. I was angry at and about a lot of things—my dad was one of them.

About three and a half years into this lifestyle, I was with my dad after church on a Saturday night, and he looked at me and said, "Hey, do you have a second to talk?" I immediately thought he was going to confront me about the double life I had been leading, but instead he said, "I want to apologize to you. I'm sorry I put the church before you." He didn't say, "I'm sorry you felt that way," or "I'm sorry you misinterpreted things and felt hurt." I felt like he truly knew what I was feeling. But in the moment, I responded flippantly: "Cool, thanks. Got to go!" I ran out of the church, got in my car, and started weeping. I didn't know it at the time, but something broke in my heart.

I continued to live the way I had been, but it was like my eyes were opened, and my heart started to soften a bit. Later that year, I was pretty deep in a toxic relationship, and I wasn't sure if I was pregnant or not. The guy I was with had gotten more and more abusive, and I was at rock bottom. I remember sitting in an empty garage and desperately praying, "God, if you want me, You can have me."

Around this time, Steve and Melody, who are family friends from church, started reaching out and asking me to have dinner with them. I had known them most of my life, but I didn't really want to spend a night talking "Christianese" and pretending I was okay. But they kept asking, so I finally relented.

We went to dinner at a local steakhouse, and they asked me about my relationship with

> **The enemy wants to keep you in darkness, but the best thing you can do is bring it to light.**

the Lord. I lied out the wazoo and thought they were totally buying it! Then, it got really quiet. I thought, *Oh no! They know.* And Steve said to me, "I have something to tell you. Ten years ago, when your dad first started the church, I had a dream. You were surrounded by darkness, and you said to the Lord, 'If you want me, You can have me.'" At nineteen years old, it all clicked. That was the moment God became personal to me. He didn't know me because of my last name or my father—He knew me and all my pain because I was *His*.

I began to confess *everything* to them—what I been going through and about the life I had been living. All the mess, all the sin. Every last detail. And then at the very end, I said, "Thanks so much for letting me share all this, but you can't help me because I've been trying to get right with God—act better, do better, not have sex—all the things I'm supposed to do. But it's not working." Then Steve responded, "We can help you, but you just helped yourself by bringing it to the light."

In looking back, I see how true Steve's comment was. With my confession, with me bringing things to light, came the first glimpses of freedom. After my confession to God, to Steve and Melody, and then later to my parents, everything started to change.

Confession isn't something we like to talk about a lot. And when we do, we tend to focus solely on confessing to God. That's essential, but through personal experience, I have to say that confessing to other people you trust is also powerful—and biblical. James 5:16 says, "Confess your sins *to each other* . . . so that you may be healed" (emphasis added). When you speak something out loud to another person, sometimes it loses its power over you. When I confessed what I had been going through, the power it had over me started to crumble. I received help, and I became free.

The enemy wants to keep you in darkness, but the best thing you can do is bring it to light.

Finding Beauty in the Mess

Is there a situation, a habit, or a problem that you feel like you can't get victory over? Confess it to the Lord today, and consider also sharing with a trusted friend or mentor.

TOOTSIE ROLLS

Elaine Fisher

"'What do these stones mean to you?' Then you shall answer them that the waters of the Jordan were cut off before the ark of the covenant of the LORD; when it crossed over the Jordan . . . And these stones shall be for a memorial to the children of Israel forever."

Joshua 4:6–7

*A*fter I told Steve and Melody about my past, we set a date for me to share everything with my parents at dinner. But before the dinner could happen, my whole family ended up at a lake house for a long weekend. That night, when no one else was around but my mom and me, she leaned across the table and asked, "Are you pregnant?" Knowing there was no point in lying anymore, I responded, "I don't know."

She got my dad, and the three of us went outside to talk, away from the rest of the family. As my dad was walking out the door, he saw a glass jar of mini Tootsie Rolls. (Mom has a major sweet tooth and always has candy around the house.) So he grabbed a handful and put them in his pocket.

We walked out to the dock, and I told them the truth about the life I'd been living. I knew I wasn't going to get out every detail, but I got to the heart of the fact that I had been rebelling and my heart was closed off to them and to God. I had been living a double life. I told them I wanted freedom from the abuse, the lies, and the sexual sin. I didn't know who I was anymore. My identity was so blurred, and there was so much mud, I couldn't tell where the foundation was. But I knew I needed to be free. And I would do anything to get there.

The conversation wasn't easy. I was shaking and bawling, and they were crying. They prayed over me and gave me big hugs, and then we all went to bed. I don't think any of us got much sleep that night, but the next morning I felt hopeful and ready for a new beginning.

I moved back home with them, and together we started the process of rebuilding my identity and my life.

A year after our conversation on the dock, my dad and I went on a dad-daughter date to a restaurant at Reunion Tower in downtown Dallas. I had always wanted to go there together, but we had never gotten the

> **God tells us to build altars or memorials to serve as a reminder of what He's done.**

chance. We ate a great dinner, and then my dad said, "I brought dessert!" (Ethan and I were dating and talking about marriage, so I instantly thought he was my "dessert" and was coming to propose to me!) But Dad reached into his jacket pocket and pulled out a mini Tootsie Roll and placed it between us. He told me how he had emptied his pockets the night I confessed everything and kept this Tootsie Roll on a tray in his room. Then he said, "The Lord told me that we're going to close one chapter tonight and that it's time to open another." We tried to eat the Tootsie Roll, but it was so stale we had to ask the waiter for steak knives. Even so, it was the best dessert I've ever had!

There's a passage in Joshua 3 where the Israelites, while carrying the Ark of the Covenant, cross the Jordan River on dry ground. It's a beautiful miracle, and in the next chapter, the Lord commands for twelve men, one from each tribe, to gather stones from the middle of the river where they crossed and build a memorial on the shores. God then says that those stones will be "a memorial to the children of Israel forever" (Joshua 4:7) of the miracle God did. I love that God told them to grab the stones from the *middle* of the river. We can easily forget, so God tells us to build altars or memorials to serve as a reminder of what He's done and to tell our children and grandchildren about them.

Tootsie Rolls are my stones of remembrance. (When they're stale, they're pretty much rocks anyway!) Every time I see a Tootsie Roll, I think about my middle-of-the-river season—the place God brought me from—and how He cleansed my heart and brought me freedom. Whenever I see a Tootsie Roll, I take a moment to remember the process it took to get where I am today and how God has redeemed me. I will not forget God's faithfulness to pull me out of that bondage and bring me into a real relationship with Him. As long as Tootsie Rolls are around and even beyond that, I will not forget.

Finding Beauty in the Mess

What are your rock reminders?
What freedoms or battles were hard-won?
What miracles do you need to establish memorials
for so you don't forget them?
Take some time today to remember God's faithfulness.

REDEMPTION STORIES

Debbie Morris

*Therefore, if anyone is in Christ, he is a new creation;
old things have passed away; behold, all things have become new.*

2 Corinthians 5:17

Innate in every parent is this thing that makes you want your kids' lives to be as perfect and painless as possible. From the moment they're born to when they get married and even beyond that, you do everything you can to protect them from hurt or harm. You train up your child in the way they should go. You provide for them. You pray for them, and you try to steer them in the right direction. But I've learned, at the end of the day, they will make their own choices, and sometimes their choices will really grieve you.

This is what happened when Elaine told us about the way she had been living and the abuse she had been experiencing from her boyfriend. It was absolutely gut-wrenching. Previously, I had a feeling she wasn't in a good place, spiritually or emotionally, but I had no clue the extent of it. She was a masterful liar. She would pop in and tell us what we wanted to hear and then go out and do whatever she wanted. Robert and I were unaware how bad it really was.

In hindsight, there were a lot of signs I wish we would have noticed and things we could have done to protect her. (Although at one time I did suggest putting a tracking device on her car!) We were so busy and distracted—Robert was traveling almost every week, and I was leading our women's ministry at church. But if we had known even a little bit of her struggle, we would have paused everything and taken more time with her.

When we first found out about the life she'd been leading, I remember being more than a little mad at Elaine for not sharing with us sooner. Even in the midst of the abuse and her sinful choices, she could have come to us. We loved her and would have protected her. But I couldn't stay mad at her because I knew it was the enemy that kept her from coming to us for so long.

> God can take the choices you've made and the hurts you've endured and use them to make something really beautiful and powerful for His glory.

Elaine's story is not of the perfect pastor's daughter or the perfect pastor's wife who lived in a little castle of perfect Christian people around her. She understands what it means to really hurt, to absolutely hit rock bottom. And those experiences, as painful as they are for me to hear and for her to experience, have made her a much better minister, mom, and friend.

As a mom, I would do anything to take away the pain she experienced. But I realize it's part of her story, and God is using it to help so many people find healing and freedom. Similarly, God has always taken the terrible messes I've experienced in my life and marriage and made them into something beautiful.

The Bible is full of stories of redemption just like hers. I think of Paul—formerly Saul of Tarsus, the feared Christian killer. He was a murderer, but God met him on the road, showed him a better way, and changed his name. Paul then became the foremost author of the New Testament. Or we could look at King David. God said he was a "man after My own heart" (Acts 13:22), but he was also an adulterer and a murderer. David often made mistakes, and God continues to use his life and story to this day. Even Rahab, who was a prostitute, believed in God and put her life on the line to help strangers escape her city. She went from the lowest of the low to being a part of the genealogy of King David and ultimately Jesus.

What's your story? We all have wounds and sins in our past, some more visible than others, but our God is a redeemer.

I've seen God redeem situations and people right in front of my eyes—Robert and Elaine and many others. God can take the choices you've made and the hurts you've endured and use them to make something really beautiful and powerful for His glory.

Maybe, like me, you're on the other side of a story like Elaine's. Are you grieving or disappointed in someone else's choices today? I've been there. God understands those feelings. Humanity has sinned and grieved God since the beginning of time. You will not be able to protect those you love from everything, even themselves. In times like that, prayer is a good weapon. Continue to contend for them in prayer. Continue to have grace for them. Continue to love them. God can turn anything around and use it for His glory—we know that anyone in Christ is a *new* creation (see 2 Corinthians 5:17). God loves your family even more than you do! And He loves to redeem and restore.

Finding Beauty in the Mess

Take a moment and thank God for your salvation and the wounds He has healed throughout your life.
If you're grieving someone else's actions today, ask the Holy Spirit to encourage your heart and tell you how to pray for them and love them well.

LOVE ALWAYS

Debbie Morris

And now abide faith, hope, love, these three;
but the greatest of these is love.

1 Corinthians 13:13

When the kids were growing up, Robert and I made a point to always tell them we loved them no matter what, no strings attached. In fact, we had a favorite saying we would repeat to each other on a regular basis: "I love you with all my heart, no matter what, forever and always!"

Sometimes Robert would go through a whole little speech with the kids. He'd say, "I'll never stop loving you." And then he'd say, "If you do something bad, I'm still going to love you." And sometimes it would turn into jokes, "Even if you steal all the candy in the world, I'm still going to love you." And he'd always end it with, "I love you with all my heart, no matter what, forever and always!" And the kids would say it back to him. It became part of our family ethos.

This started early on in our marriage when Robert and I began learning a lot about grace and exploring more of who God is. We both had an idea, a sense, of what it was like to live under unyielding law, but once we had a revelation of the incredible love and grace that God has for us, we wanted to convey it to our kids. We wanted them to know we were going to strive to love them in the same way God loves us.

With two boys and Elaine in the house, this family phrase was definitely tested, but never so much as when Elaine was a teenager. When she finally told us about her past and all the things she had gotten involved in, we were shocked and disappointed. But we also sought to be gracious and loving throughout the healing season, just as we knew God had been for us at various times in our lives. It was difficult at times as we got to know more about her past, and we may have given her a lecture (or several), but she always knew she was loved. And she told us recently that she never doubted that for a second.

Yet I know that as intentional as Robert and I were with the kids, we still fell short of the enormity of God's grace

> There's no surprising Him with your past, and there's no bank of love and grace and mercy you have to build up with Him in order to draw from it when you mess up.

and love for us. My love for my husband and children is great, but it's still just a fraction of what the Lord's love is for you and me.

God loves us unconditionally and *always* has more than enough grace available. It's immediate. He already knows everything about you and loves you completely! There's no surprising Him with your past, and there's no bank of love and grace and mercy you have to build up with Him in order to draw from it when you mess up—it's just who He is! And He offers His love and grace without hesitation. Have you received this truth? Because when you accept this incredible truth, you are empowered to share it with others.

I want to encourage you today to receive God's love for you, and in return, love others deeply and give grace freely, not just in your words but in your actions. Ephesians 5:1 says, "Therefore be imitators of God as dear children. And walk in love, as Christ also has loved us and given Himself for us, an offering and a sacrifice to God for a sweet-smelling aroma."

You can be a mirror of Christ's love, even when it's hard, when it's a sacrifice, and when things aren't turning out the way you expected. I know firsthand what that feels like. Thankfully, God promises to help us do this! I pray the Lord will give you full knowledge of His grace today and the supernatural power to love others without hesitation as you remember that He loves you with all His heart, no matter what, forever and always!

Finding Beauty in the Mess

Have you received God's incredible love?
Is there someone you need to show love or grace to today,
even if it's difficult?

HOW TO EAT AN ELEPHANT

Elaine Fisher

*In my distress I prayed to the L*ORD*,
and the L*ORD *answered me and set me free.*

Psalm 118:5 (NLT)

*T*here's a famous proverb that goes: How do you eat an elephant? *One bite at a time.*

I kept telling myself this as I confessed to my double life and prepared for the stepping stones to get out of the toxic, abusive relationship and lifestyle I had entangled myself in for so many years.

It wasn't easy. I had tried to get out other times. I knew it was an abusive relationship, but every time I tried to get out, there was something that roped me back in. It was a toxic, mental game. And, because there was sex involved, I had a soul tie that kept me bound. I felt I had to stay because of how deeply we were involved. Not to mention, he was a phenomenal apologizer, as most abusers are. Each time he apologized, I thought, *Oh, okay, everything is about to change! It'll be fine now.* But nothing ever changed, and I would always feel foolish for thinking things would be different.

For three years, my life had been so tightly controlled by this man. I didn't do much without his permission. When I brought my family into my double life and started to pursue a life that honored God, they helped me break off from this relationship.

After leaving him, Mom and I started by clearing out my closet of any clothes that reminded me of him, which ended up being 97 percent of my wardrobe. About a week later, my dad came to me and read the story of the prodigal son. After he finished, he asked, "What did the father do?" I said, "He gave the son a hug?" And my dad said, "No, he threw the son a party! Let's go to New York and get a new wardrobe for you."

The following week, my dad preached on a Tuesday night and recorded the message to play on the weekend so we could travel to New York together. This was the first time he had ever pre-recorded a message to play on the weekend, and I knew he did it intentionally to heal my heart from believing he valued the

> **Your path to freedom may look different than you expected.**

church more than me and to celebrate that I came home—to my parents and to the Lord.

For the rest of the year, I did anything I needed to get free. I was so broken and didn't know who I was, so I relied on my parents for guidance in rebuilding myself. I willingly did everything they asked of me. In a practical sense, this included changing my phone number and even getting rid of my phone altogether for a season, deleting my social media accounts, giving them my car keys, and communicating where I was going any time I went somewhere without them. I knew I couldn't trust myself or my ex if I had those things available to me.

I also traveled full-time with my dad and went to every service with him. We spent a lot of time together, which was so healing for my broken heart. We even went to counseling together and worked through a lot of anger and hurt. It was a big deal to me that he was willing to talk to someone else about my feelings and our relationship. He even apologized and owned certain things he had done wrong along the way.

This may not sound like freedom to you, but it was to me! Not only did I need to remove myself from an abusive relationship and any temptation to go back, I needed to heal. I also began to experience a relationship with God outside of my parents and my church culture, and it was so refreshing! This process was my way of eating the elephant one bite at a time.

Why am I telling you all of this? Because your path to freedom may look different than you expected. My path didn't include exercise, bubble baths, and lots of journaling with candles nearby. Yours might. But mine included no phone and my parents driving me everywhere. It was messy, and it took a long time. I had to do things I didn't want to do. Some people were even confused about why I was doing or not doing certain things. But these were my stepping stones to freedom and healing, and I was more than willing to do them.

Whatever freedom or healing you need, I want to encourage you to take it step by step and know that the things you do may be different from the things other people do to experience healing. Naaman had to wash in a river seven times (see 2 Kings 5:1-19), while King Hezekiah prayed and used figs to be healed (see 2 Kings 20:1-7). Jesus healed one person with a touch, another by putting spit and mud on his eyes, and another with just the hem of His robe. While these are examples of physical healing and freedom, I think the same applies to spiritual healing and freedom. Listen to the Holy Spirit's leading. Your story might not look like someone else's. Your story might take time. But how you eat an elephant is the same—one bite at a time.

Finding Beauty in the Mess

What freedom or healing are you longing for in your life?
What is the Holy Spirit saying to you about your next step?

YOUR BEST FRIEND

Debbie Morris

"No longer do I call you servants, for a servant does not know what his master is doing; but I have called you friends."

John 15:15

*E*laine and I are best friends. Yes, we're mother and daughter. Yes, we're decades apart in age. And yes, we're best friends. But it hasn't always been this way.

As parents, there were many years when we were *not* our children's friends. When the kids were young, we had to discipline them and guide them and tell them not to do things that may harm them. We set boundaries and said "no" when they were approaching a cliff, both real and figurative. We had to be the boss.

Yet even in those early years, Robert and I worked hard to lay a foundation for friendship in the future. We tried to find common ground with each of our kids. As they got older, we began to transition out of the boss role and move into a coach role. Sometimes this meant trusting them to make good choices when all we really wanted to do was protect them or control a situation. There were some tough days!

With Elaine, it wasn't until she was saved at nineteen and started to be vulnerable about what she was going through that our relationship began to change. I asked questions and let her process things. I still gave advice, but I let her come to her own conclusions. Things shifted from "you must do this, and you must follow these rules" to "if you don't take my advice, that's on you, not me. I'm not holding you to it, but I will always give it." It changed even more when she got married and started having her own kids.

As she continued to follow God and make good decisions, it was fun to transition from coach to being her cheerleader and friend. She reciprocated the friendship that I wanted with her. It wasn't just me wanting that relationship—she chose it too. And it's been so special for both of us. We seldom go a day without talking on the phone or texting or planning a visit to see one another.

This may sound obvious, but relationships change. And that's okay. They're meant to change. The way that you interact with your parents or your kids or

> **He wants to be your Lord and Savior, but as you grow in maturity, He also wants to be your friend.**

your siblings will change over the years. Similarly, your relationship with the Lord should change and progress, too.

God wants you to mature in your faith and knowledge of Christ so you're not easily influenced or "tossed and blown about by every wind of new teaching" (Ephesians 4:13–14 NLT). He wants to be your Lord and Savior, but as you grow in maturity, He also wants to be your friend. Moses was intentional to meet with God regularly in the tent of meeting, and the Bible later says he talked with God as with a friend (see Exodus 33:11). Abraham was also called God's friend (see James 2:23). And Jesus said in John 15:14–15, "You are My friends if you do whatever I command you. No longer do I call you servants, for a servant does not know what his master is doing; but I have called you friends, for all things that I heard from My Father I have made known to you."

It's no mistake that Jesus called the disciples His friends shortly after saying, "Abide in Me . . . I am the vine, you are the branches" (John 15:4–5). As you are intentional to obey what God says and abide in Him, your relationship will shift to a deep and loving friendship.

We will never stop needing our good Father to guide us through life. We will never stop being His children. But being His friend is special too. I want to encourage you to keep diving into the Word, keep listening to the Holy Spirit, and keep living out your faith. And if you view God as only Lord or only Savior or only Father, I want to encourage you to broaden your perspective to also see Him as your Friend—your best Friend.

Finding Beauty in the Mess

Do you view Jesus as your friend?
What can you do today to be intentional about building
your relationship with Him?

WHO IS IN THE GARDEN WITH YOU?

Elaine Fisher

One who has unreliable friends soon comes to ruin,
but there is a friend who sticks closer than a brother.

Proverbs 18:24 (NIV)

When I was younger, I didn't know how to choose my friends. I knew how to *make* friends, but I didn't know how to *choose* friends. I let them choose me, and I just went along with everything. And when things got tough or toxic, I didn't know how to break up with friends and find new ones. So after I pleaded with them, my parents would pull me out of public school and send me to a private school or try homeschooling me. (The homeschooling thing never lasted long. I talked nonstop, and Mom said

41

she needed me to go back to school so she could have her sanity back.)

But no matter where I went, I somehow landed in the midst of all the wrong people. I didn't know how to pursue healthy friendships or create boundaries for myself. The Bible says that "bad company corrupts good character" (1 Corinthians 15:33 NLT). Ain't that the truth! I didn't understand that I had a choice. And out of all those toxic friendships, I was the common denominator. I let other people think for me, and I ended up having friends *in* certain circumstances instead of having friends who would help me *through* circumstances. It was an unstable, inconsistent, and sometimes painful way to live.

Now, I choose my friends wisely.

There's no doubt in my mind that humans were created to live in community with other people. Having friends is so important—even Jesus had friends! But the older I get, the more I realize I don't want to just choose people I can have fun with or who "get" me. Those things are great! But I want a community that will support and encourage me through *any* circumstance, not just be there for the good stuff. I want friends who are not gossips—who don't want to know about my life to just know about it. I want people in my life who I am equally yoked with and who can speak wisdom and God's Word into my life.

> I ended up having friends *in* certain circumstances instead of having friends who would help me *through* circumstances.

Our culture makes it seem like you can have hundreds of great friends or none at all. But I'm not sure either of those routes is healthy or even feasible. I like to look at Jesus' relationships while He was here on earth. He had varying levels of friendships, and I believe He intentionally and strategically chose the people He wanted to be around Him. Most scholars say Jesus chose three core friends (Peter, James, and John) who were with Him most of the time. He then had the twelve disciples who were often close to Him, a larger group of followers He enjoyed company with and poured into, and then a crowd of acquaintances. The access and vulnerability the core friends and disciples experienced with Jesus was different than the rest of the His followers and the crowd.

Peter, James, and John saw the highs and the lows of Jesus' earthly ministry. They saw the majority of Jesus' miracles firsthand and also accompanied Him on the mountain where He was transfigured in front of them (see Matthew 17:1–8). They were invited deeper into the Garden of Gethsemane with Him, moments before His arrest, when He pleaded with God and prayed until "His sweat became like great drops of blood falling down to the ground" (Luke 22:44). Jesus even entrusted His mother into John's care upon His death on the cross. Although we can't know exactly what their friendship looked like or if it's similar to our modern view of friendship, most people believe the Son of God had close friends—an inner circle of people around Him.

Who are those core friends for you? Who are the people you can call up and say, "I'm going through something," and they will sit close and pray with you through it?

I know that finding these kinds of friends is difficult at times. I want to encourage you to pray for wisdom to choose the right friends. I have decided I'm not going to simply let someone into the intimate, vulnerable spiritual warfare moments of my life because their kids go to the same school as mine or we work together and their friendship is convenient. I appreciate that kind of acquaintance, and maybe one of those people will become a close friend later on, but it will take time. I don't let my circumstances define who my friends are anymore. My circumstances may define who I hang out with during a certain season, but that doesn't mean they're coming into the garden with me. This may sound harsh or like having a friend for a season is bad, but as someone who has let convenient friends dictate her life in the past, it's important for me to establish and maintain stable, solid, godly friendships. Truth is, it's important for all of us.

We're not meant to go through life alone, but we can choose who we take along for the journey.

Finding Beauty in the Mess

Think about the friendships you have right now.
Do you have stick-with-you friends or circumstantial,
bad-influence friends? If you don't have any core friends or the
right kinds of friends right now, ask the Lord to bring them to
you! He is faithful to bring you good, healthy friendships.

TWO KIDS PLAYING HOUSE

Debbie Morris

We can rejoice, too, when we run into problems and trials,
for we know that they help us develop endurance.
And endurance develops strength of character,
and character strengthens our confident hope of salvation.
And this hope will not lead to disappointment.
For we know how dearly God loves us, because he has given us
the Holy Spirit to fill our hearts with his love.

Romans 5:3–5 (NLT)

I have always said I met Robert in the fifth grade, but Robert is sure we met in sixth. I guess I just like to imagine more of my life with him in it! We attended the same church and youth group, but we really didn't know each other. I'd even say we were worlds apart. I was quiet and a rule keeper, and he was never far from trouble.

In spite of our differences, when I was seventeen and Robert was sixteen, he asked me out. At the end of our date, we were standing on the back porch, and I was fidgeting with a hanging plant. My dad opened the back door and said, "Deb, it's time to come in." Embarrassed, I quickly responded, "I'll be right there!" But before I turned to go inside, Robert kissed me goodnight, and I fell in love.

While it was a *really* good kiss, one kiss isn't enough for a lifetime. Robert and I have had our ups and downs throughout the years. Marriage isn't easy. Ministry isn't easy. Life isn't easy. And it's really not easy when your spouse is unfaithful.

It was life-shaking, and in the almost forty years since, it is still one of the more difficult seasons of my life. It was my first time to navigate something so serious as an adult—just me and God. This could have easily broken us, but I was stubborn enough not to go back to my parents' house. I wasn't going to be a two- or three-year marriage dropout. And Robert was (and continues to be) a fantastic father—I wasn't going to separate our son from his father.

The night Robert confessed to me what had happened, we were staying in a hotel, and after he shared with me, I grabbed the Gideons

> The way God blessed us through that situation gives me confidence that He will work out every other difficulty I experience in my life for good.

Bible from the nightstand and fled to the bathroom. It was the only place to go. I cried and read the Word and prayed for most of the night. God showed up for me that night and every day after that. He gave me grace. I found new mercies for each new day, and I realized I was going to be stronger and better on the other side of this.

I watched us both change. I watched our marriage change. That season, as hard and messy as it was, made us better. God made us better. We were just two kids playing house until that happened. We had to learn to really communicate, how to be transparent with one another—how to be *married*. Honestly, what the Lord brought out of it was so much better than what I could have ever imagined. I can now trace a lot of the good foundations in our marriage back to that season, and I'm truly grateful. Not for Robert's actions, but for the good fruit that was produced in our lives.

I married my high school sweetheart, and our lives together have never really made sense. But I have seen God do miracles in us (the fact that we still *really* like each other all these years later is one of them!), and I have even greater trust in Him now. The way God blessed us through that situation gives me confidence that He will work out every other difficulty I experience in my life for good.

There may be a lot in your world that doesn't make sense—your marriage, your job, your family, the trials you've endured—but maybe it's in those moments of "this doesn't make sense" or "this is not what I envisioned for my life" that God is doing something important. While I would never wish for anyone to have a husband who was unfaithful, I do hope you see God create something incredible out of even your worst moments.

Are you disappointed today? Are you frustrated with how your life is unfolding so far? Are you navigating a trial or difficulty? I encourage you, *do not lose hope*! Second Corinthians 4:16–18 says, "Therefore we do not lose heart. . . . For our light affliction, which is but for a moment, is working for us a far more exceeding and eternal weight of glory, while we do not look at the things which are seen, but at the things which are not seen. For the things which are seen are temporary, but the things which are not seen are eternal."

God loves you dearly, and He has good, eternal things planned for you that you may not see right now. Do not lose heart. Maybe, like me and Robert—the boy I've loved since our first kiss—God is building a foundation for something sweet and strong.

Finding Beauty in the Mess

What is the Lord saying to you about your circumstances?
Trust that God is with you today and working to create
something beautiful.

A SLOW MURDER

Elaine Fisher

Two are better than one,
because they have a good reward for their labor.
For if they fall, one will lift up his companion.
And a threefold cord is not quickly broken.

Ecclesiastes 4:9–10, 12

Shortly after Ethan and I got married, my mom and I were talking about a frustration I had with him. She shared about a time she had been in a similar situation with my dad. I remember a moment of relief washing over me as I said, "Oh, you get annoyed with your husband too?!" And I thought, *Whew, okay, I'm normal.*

I went into married life thinking it would be easy because we both loved Jesus and Ethan was "the one." Then we hit trials and had arguments and bursts of frustration, and I began to wonder if maybe we weren't as compatible as I'd thought. I expected our marriage to look like my parents', but they had been married for close to thirty years. I was expecting a foundation to be there that Ethan and I hadn't built yet! My biggest fault in marriage has been my expectations. (Our premarital counselor told me this, and I just laughed! Apparently, it was true.) Now, thirteen years in, I'm still reworking my expectations.

We live in a time where social media is a big deal. I believe it's actually guiding our culture, and within it, there's a lot of talk about what *we* deserve, what makes *us* comfortable, how to meet *our* needs, and *self*-care. I recognize taking time for yourself and not letting people walk all over you is necessary, but more and more, the rhetoric often leans toward complete selfishness. If we're not careful, self-care can become self-indulgence. We can even become entitled and demand that our self be cared for first.

Social media feeds us unreal or even wrong expectations for what our lives are supposed to look like. We see a twenty second clip of someone's seemingly perfect life and the flowers her husband brought home and images that compel us to compare our bodies, our homes, and our marriages. We develop unrealistic expectations, and I believe, as a result, we're seeing a lot more divorces in the younger

> **If we're not careful, self-care can become self-indulgence.**

generation, because it's just not what they assumed marriage would be.

Ethan is truly a gift to me, but I jokingly told the Lord early on in our marriage that this gift feels like a slow murder. But in a good way! The Lord calls us to die in order to live (see Luke 9:23–25; Galatians 5:24). And with every little death of self, I've grown and lived more fully. My marriage is often the catalyst for that. It's caused me to find my voice and forced me to do a lot of good things. Ethan challenges me more than anyone. He prays for me more than anyone. He loves me like no one else. And I do the same with him.

Jesus showed us how to care for the people in our lives—we are called to *serve*. When Ethan and I focus on serving one another and God together, we have a great time being married! It took time to build a strong foundation and find our groove as a couple and a family. But when we try to compete with one another or focus on our selfish needs, our unrealistic expectations, and our differences, we experience annoyance and frustration.

Over the years, I have reframed my thinking to see our differences as complementary instead of contradictory. I've become accustomed to the death of selfishness. I've seen that we are much better together than on our own. And I know that ultimately, Ethan and I are together so we can sharpen each other and help each other look more like Christ so God can do something amazing through us. I envision God using our marriage to reach people. Together, we can fulfill God's call to be an image of Christ's love to a lost and hurting world.

My marriage isn't perfect by any means, but I'm not going to let selfishness, false expectations, or the comparison of others sully what a gift my marriage is and what God is going to do through us.

What expectations about your relationships do you need to examine today? Are you letting social media or other people tell you what they should look like? Have you bought into the enemy's lies of selfishness? Take some time with the Lord today to ask Him about His desire for your relationships.

Finding Beauty in the Mess

Is there an area of your life where you've let selfishness, comparison, or unreal expectations win? Bring it to the Lord, and ask Him how He sees your circumstances or relationships.

WHAT DO YOU REALLY MEAN?

Debbie Morris

And behold, the LORD passed by, and a great and strong
wind tore into the mountains
and broke the rocks in pieces before the LORD,
but the LORD was not in the wind;
and after the wind an earthquake,
but the LORD was not in the earthquake;
and after the earthquake a fire, but the LORD was not in the fire;
and after the fire a still small voice.

1 Kings 19:11–12

When you've been married as long as Robert and I have, you develop a sort of synchronization of routine. The systems work. There's a give and take. He knows you don't like numbers, and you know he will pay the electricity bill. But there are still seasons when you come across your differences. And as Robert and I have explored those things together, we've become even closer.

Our latest realization involved our communication. You see, my dad was famous for his grunts. He would grunt "ugh," and I knew he wanted iced tea. He'd grunt "eht" at the dining table, and I knew he needed salt, so I'd get the salt for him. He'd grunt "hah," and I knew that meant he needed a particular set of pliers. It was this crazy little way my dad communicated. He was very intelligent and gifted; he just wasn't extremely verbal. And throughout the years, I learned to interpret what each grunt meant and then respond accordingly.

Eventually, I grew up and married Robert, who is a very articulate and verbal person. And he communicates to me exactly what he wants. He says what he wants and means what he says. But that wasn't how I was hearing it. For four decades, I would ask myself, *What is he really saying?* I would try to decipher what he *really* meant or needed and respond with something totally different than what he said. This was exasperating and frustrating for both of us! I was often stressed trying to figure out some hidden meaning behind what he was saying. And Robert was often frustrated when I misunderstood him.

> **The way the Lord communicates with you may be different than how He communicates with someone else.**

It wasn't until we were almost forty-one years into our marriage that we discovered why we sometimes had trouble communicating. I had spent my whole childhood trying to discern what the main man in my life wanted from a *grunt*. And I didn't realize I had been doing this with my husband's words too!

Once Robert and I had this epiphany, our communication and understanding of one another changed. I'm learning to take him at his literal word. And he has more grace for me when he says something and I interpret it differently. We can even laugh about it now. We're still learning—even forty-one years in!

This is an amusing story, but I think we sometimes do this when we communicate with God and allow things from our past to skew how we perceive Him, hear from Him, or interpret His Word.

I'm reminded of a passage in 1 Kings 19 where Elijah has an encounter with God, but God doesn't show up for Elijah in the way we would expect. He's not in the mighty wind or the earthquake or the fire, but in a still, small voice. I love this passage because it tells me to ease my expectations when God is speaking to me and not to overthink it.

Obviously, the Holy Spirit speaks to us in any way He wants to, and I've received Scriptures, pictures, and impressions from Him over the years. But most often, I feel Him speak through a sense of peace. And when considering options or a decision, I operate on that peace. Whereas Robert is more prone to have a Scripture—book, chapter, and verse—of what he feels the Holy Spirit is speaking to him. All this to say, the way the Lord communicates with you may be different than how He communicates with someone else. The way my dad communicated with me is different than the way Robert does! There's no right or wrong answer.

It's never too late to learn more about your relationship with God. I want to encourage you to think about how God speaks to you and how you interpret what He says. You may discover how the Lord communicates with you is not the way you expected or experienced in the past.

Finding Beauty in the Mess

Have you been letting things from your past skew the way you perceive God, hear from Him, or interpret His Word? Let the Holy Spirit bring those things to mind and share with you His truth.

OPEN HANDS

Elaine Fisher

*Get rid of all bitterness, rage, anger, harsh words, and slander,
as well as all types of evil behavior. Instead, be kind to each other,
tenderhearted, forgiving one another, just as God through
Christ has forgiven you.*

Ephesians 4:31–32 (NLT)

Three years into my marriage, I was ready for babies. I *really* wanted to get pregnant, and I was disappointed and frustrated it wasn't happening as quickly as I hoped.

During this time, I traveled to Greece to teach at a women's conference with a few well-known Christian leaders. Shortly after arriving, my friend Tom came to visit. (Tom is my funny way of saying, "time of the month." But I wasn't laughing.) This was just another reminder I was still not pregnant. The waiting was excruciating, and I was beginning to feel hopeless.

The night before the conference, a few of us gathered together and decided to take a moment to pray for the person next to us. I quickly realized I was seated next to Lisa Bevere, a well-known speaker and author and incredible woman of God. I felt intimidated having to pray for someone I look up to, and when we huddled together to pray, she said, "You go first." So I nervously prayed a simple prayer for her. Then she began to pray for me. She put her hand on my stomach and began to prophetically speak life and healing over me. When the prayer ended, we went our separate ways, but I met God in that moment. God used her prayers to remind me that He saw me in the middle of my journey to motherhood.

The next day, I approached Lisa because I wanted to share how God had used her the night before, but before I could get my words out, she said, "I have a word for you I need to share. There's someone in your past you need to forgive. God wants to give you the desires of your heart, but your hands are full of bitterness." My mind was flooded with memories of my abusive ex-boyfriend. Shocked and angry, I told her I had a righteous anger because what he did was wrong.

While Lisa didn't know the details of my past, she took a moment to listen and gently reminded me that unforgiveness is

> I believe the other side of forgiveness holds a gift.

more about *me* than him. She told me that my unforgiveness was holding me back, and my choice to forgive him did not mean reconciliation or that what he did was right. Instead, forgiveness sets me free. It gives God access to that part of my heart, so He can heal it and use it for His glory.

As I sat with her words, I thought I would give it a shot. That day, I made a choice to go on a journey to forgive this man who had hurt me very deeply. Every day I would say, "Today, I choose to forgive." As time went on, that got easier to say, and I felt heaviness lifting off me. To my surprise, a year later, I got pregnant.

Six weeks into my pregnancy, I started bleeding. The doctors told me I had a tear in my placenta that would bleed out and I would miscarry. Immediately, I was tempted to doubt God. I was tempted to blame all of this on my past and the abuse I went through. But as Ethan was praying over me and declaring Scripture over us and our unborn child, I remembered I had a choice. In the midst of the pain, grief, and unknown, I remember saying, "God, I choose to forgive. I trust You, and even if I miscarry, You are still faithful."

By the grace of God, Adde was born full-term, and I had no other complications during my pregnancy. After she was born, the doctor showed me a scar on my placenta and said, "It looks like someone stitched your placenta back together. Did you have surgery?" And as I said, "No, I didn't," I knew it was the hand of God that stitched my placenta together and saved my child.

I know my story may bring up many different emotions for people. Some of you may be walking through something similar. I want to make sure you know that not all hardship in life is because of unforgiveness or sin. We live in a fallen world. Sometimes, we go through things that don't make sense, and we may never have the answers we desire.

I share my story because I believe the other side of forgiveness holds a gift. While you may feel righteous in your anger, unforgiveness is only damaging you. I know this is a hard choice to make, and I don't ask you to make it so you can demand God give you a gift on the other side. I ask you to forgive so you can be healed, whole, and ready for God to do something through you. I hope you will come to a place where, in the midst of pain, grief, and the unknown, you can say, "God, even if this doesn't go how I want it to go, You remain faithful."

So today, take a moment to make the hard decision to forgive—not for them but for you! You never know what might be the catalyst for your breakthrough, your healing, or your victory. Open your hands and see what He does.

Finding Beauty in the Mess

Have you been holding bitterness and unforgiveness
toward someone? You can choose today
to open your hands and forgive.

SOUR CANDY IN THE DESERT

Debbie Morris

I press on to reach the end of the race and receive the heavenly prize for which God, through Christ Jesus, is calling us.

Philippians 3:14 (NLT)

When the kids were young, we used to go on long road trips as a family. We saw some beautiful sights and had some fun family times, but there were also long stretches of road that were boring or difficult. If you've ever taken the drive from Texas to California, you know there's a whole lotta nothin' on the way. Just some deserts, unexpected potholes, and a lot of distance between rest stops.

On those trips, we sometimes drove through the night. And when it got really late and I was driving, I would eat sour candy. I *hate* sour candy, but I'd eat them (often with tears in my eyes) to stay awake. Sometimes I'd tap my face to make sure I didn't fall asleep. Sometimes I would open the windows to let in the cool night air. Sometimes I would sing a song! (The kids didn't like that because I'm not a great singer!) But I did anything I needed to stay awake on the road.

Life is like a long road trip. Even when you're headed in the right direction, sometimes you're going to drive through a desert. Sometimes you're going to get really bored. Sometimes you're going to drive down some streets that aren't pleasant and are full of potholes. It doesn't mean you're lost or doing something wrong. You don't drive through a desert and think, *Something is wrong with my car!* No, it's just part of the journey. Even Jesus spent time in a wilderness (see Matthew 4:1–11), and you know who was whispering in His ear? The enemy.

The enemy likes to find us when it's getting late, and we're tired and vulnerable and there are miles of desert around. He likes to whisper lies to us about ourselves and the Lord. The enemy wants us to question God's love for us or our salvation. The enemy wants us to fall asleep on the road or even just quit driving altogether. But it's during those late nights that you need to rely on the truth of God's Word, eat some sour candy, and keep driving through!

> **The enemy likes to find us when it's getting late, and we're tired and vulnerable and there are miles of desert around.**

When you realize you're driving in a desert where the rest stops are going to be few and far between, you need to check your provisions. Do you have water (or in my case, Dr Pepper)? Do you have snacks? Do you have gas for the car? Do you have enough phone battery in case of an emergency? You need to make sure you have resourced yourself to keep going.

So many people, when they realize they're in a desert season in life or in their relationships, pull back or turn inward. But to make it through this part of the road trip of life, you really need to pay attention. You need to map out where the next rest stop is. And when you find it, you make sure to pull in and stock up, even if you don't need those things right away. You fill your gas tank to the brim. Maybe you even close your eyes for a few minutes. Then you get in the car and keep going.

This reality about life and road trips can also apply to your relationship with the Lord. He never leaves our side, but some seasons you'll feel really close to Him, and some seasons you'll feel distant. It doesn't mean there's sin or something is wrong. Sometimes it's just part of the journey. There is an ebb and flow, and you need to keep believing, keep investing, keep driving. And I can say from experience that things feel so much sweeter when you come out on the other side.

Today, whether you're in a desert, you're approaching one, or you're coming out of one, what are the things you need to do to stay awake and engaged on the road? Maybe it's switching up the Bible version you read or changing up the music you listen to while getting ready. What provisions do you need? Maybe you need to schedule time to get away with the Lord or your spouse and spend extra time with one another. Ask the Holy Spirit to encourage and resource you with what you need for the road ahead.

The desert won't last forever. You *will* drive out of it. You *will* get back to lush greenery and consistent rest stops and newly paved roads. Until then, get out your sour candy and keep driving.

Finding Beauty in the Mess

The drive may be imperfect,
but there is beauty on the other side.
What do you need to do to persevere and keep going?

WILL YOU OBEY?

Elaine Fisher

> *[Jesus] replied, "Blessed rather are those who hear the word of God and obey it."*
>
> Luke 11:28 (NIV)

When God called Ethan and me to plant a church in Houston, I thought He had lost His mind. It all started one night when we invited my parents over for dinner. Ethan and I were on staff at Gateway at the time, and I wanted to discuss some things that were going on at the church.

During the conversation, I asked my dad, "Where do you see Ethan in the next five years?" Secretly, I was frustrated because I knew what my future was at the church, but I wasn't sure about Ethan's. So I wanted us all to get on the same page. To my surprise, my dad said, "Well, I've never really heard what Ethan wants to do." All heads turned toward

Ethan, and he said, "If I'm honest, I feel like God has called me to be a senior pastor." This was news to me! (Well, to be fair, he had told me this when we were dating, but I wasn't a big fan of the idea, so I had forgotten it and moved on. And I thought he had, too!)

Later that night, after my parents prayed over us and left, I turned to Ethan and said, "What did you just sign us up for?!" I was not interested in being church planters or lead pastors.

Growing up a pastor's kid, I saw a lot of spiritual warfare in our family. I saw my dad have multiple accidents, and almost die a couple of times from health issues. And even though I knew God was always going to take care of him and those things weren't going to kill him, I was so mad that we had to walk through any of it. I didn't want that kind of target on our backs. In my mind, the benefits of being senior pastors didn't outweigh the trouble.

Ethan's calling to be a senior pastor put a wrench in our future. I didn't expect it, I didn't want it, and I was frustrated. Deep down I knew this was the Lord, but I still had some healing to do from my past and was struggling with a lot of fear.

For three years, I wrestled with God. We had a lot of arguments and vent sessions. Mostly it was me saying, "God, You better change Ethan's mind because this is a very dumb idea." I didn't doubt Ethan's

> **Maybe God is taking you there so you can see how big He truly is.**

ability to be a senior pastor. I just didn't want that life for our family. And I didn't want to move away from the family and the ministry I loved.

One evening in the middle of this season, we attended a night of worship and sang the song "So Will I." I remember weeping as I was singing about how if creation obeys God, then I should too. And in that moment, I felt like the Lord said to me, "Do you really believe that?" I responded, "Of course, God, I'm singing it!" And I knew God was asking me to trust Him and follow His leading. We were for sure moving to Houston—three hundred miles away from my family!

After the service, I was talking to another pastor who knew we were considering a move, and he said, "You're fearful because you don't understand how big your God is. Maybe God is taking you there so you can see how big He truly is."

That was more than six years ago, and this has proved to be true. I have had many moments since where I've thought, *God, why in the world did I almost let fear stop me from this?* It's because I've seen how big He is! I've seen the hand of God move more than ever. And Ethan and I have both grown exponentially, both as a couple and individually, since moving. I don't know if we would have gotten that growth had we stayed. This doesn't mean I didn't genuinely grieve the transition or that it wasn't really hard. I went into it kicking and screaming. But obeying God has been so worth it.

Have you ever experienced this? Has God ever called you to do something that didn't make sense or that you didn't want to do? Has He ever called your spouse or family to do something and you weren't on board?

I wanted a comfortable, convenient Christian life. You may want one too. It sounds nice. But I'm sorry to tell you that I don't think anyone gets one. God has big things ahead for each of us, and in order to get there, we are going to have to leave things behind, we are going to have to face some fears, and we are going to have to put on our big girl pants and obey what He says. Because if creation, the stars and mountains and streams, obey Him, we should too.

Finding Beauty in the Mess

What has God been telling you to do that you've been resisting? Are you ready to lay down your will and be obedient to His calling?

SEASONS CHANGE

Debbie Morris

To everything there is a season,
a time for every purpose under heaven.

Ecclesiastes 3:1

Soon after Robert and I started Gateway Church, he came home one day and said, "Honey, we're starting small groups at church, and we're going to have women's groups." I responded, "Great!" And he came back with, "And you're going to lead them!" I had led the women's groups at our previous church, and I thought I was done with that. I told Robert so, but he really wanted me to think about it. Reluctantly, I volunteered to lead the women's groups for six months—*only* six months!

Well, many years later, I was still leading women's groups, but it had morphed into something even bigger—a full-blown women's ministry! Gateway was growing rapidly, and the women's ministry was thriving. But Robert and I were so busy—he was often traveling to speak, and I usually went with him. I found my attention divided, and I was overwhelmed. Our kids were teenagers and young adults at the time, and I started to feel like I should let someone else take leadership so I could be more attentive at home, specifically to Elaine. So I resigned. We had a logical person in mind to lead in my stead, so we handed the reins to her.

About a year or so after stepping away, I attended a women's ministry event at the church, and at lunch the next day, I realized I felt renewed vision and passion for women's ministry. After sharing this with Robert, he asked me to lead it again. This time, I was excited and enthusiastically said, "Yes!"

This season of ministry felt different. I discovered I really loved interacting with the ladies and planning our events and seeing God move. Life was still incredibly busy, but I experienced joy throughout this time. I felt a real burden from the Lord for women's ministry, which was different than when I was leading it earlier. Before, I was filling a need, doing what I could to help. This time, it was my choice to step back in. I took on the call, and I chose to invest in it.

Then, just a few years ago, I started to hear from the Lord that it was time to hand off the ministry

> **Are you in a season of duty and obligation or a season of passion and vision?**

to the next generation. It wasn't a feeling of, *Should I leave?* like the previous time. It was, *God is telling me to leave.* Internally, I started looking at every woman who walked past me and would pray, *Lord, is this her?* I waited for Him to say who would lead after me. I had my own ideas and thoughts on who it might be (specifically Elaine before she moved to Houston), but after a while, God spoke to me, *Bridgette.*

Bridgette is my daughter-in-law, and I knew we shared a passion for women's ministry. She's creative and energetic and works with excellence. I knew the nuances of how I would do ministry were subject to some change based on our personalities and generational differences, but I also knew she could carry on the vision God had given me for Gateway women. The transition went very smoothly, and I'm thrilled with how she's leading!

I'm so grateful for *all* the time I spent leading the women's ministry, but I can see now how these two seasons of leading and leaving were different. The first few years I led, I was doing it out of obligation, out of duty. There was a need, and I filled it. And no doubt, there's something sacrificial and beautiful about serving in that way for a time. But I was overwhelmed, and I didn't have a burden or passion for it.

The second time I was leading the women's ministry was so much more rewarding. I was doing the exact same thing as before, but this time, my heart was in it. It was something I desired to be part of, so when God told me to pass it on, in some ways it was much more difficult to do. But in other ways, it was so much easier because it was God's anointed time.

Are you in a season of duty and obligation or a season of passion and vision? We will all experience both, but it's important to recognize the difference. Ecclesiastes 3:1–8 talks about seasons: "A time to plant, and a time to pluck what is planted; . . . a time to break down, and a time to build up; a time to weep, and a time to laugh . . ." Are you planting or plucking? Breaking or building? Saying hello or saying goodbye? As you identify your season, I hope you see God's hand working in it. Whichever season you find yourself in, I pray you would learn to embrace it and whatever God is teaching you through it.

Finding Beauty in the Mess

What season are you in today? Ask the Lord to show you and give you the strength to see it through.

KEEP SHOWING UP

Elaine Fisher

Jesus replied, "You do not realize now what I am doing, but later you will understand."

John 13:7 (NIV)

*B*efore we moved to Houston, my mom was mentoring me to take the leadership role of the women's ministry at Gateway. I had been on that trajectory for seven years. I had received prophetic words about women's ministry, and I was excited to take my mom's mantle and carry it to the next generation.

And then, *Houston*.

Beyond the fact that I didn't want us to be senior pastors, I was genuinely devastated that moving there disqualified me from what I had been working toward for *seven* years! I was given a vision, and I was working toward it. I had heard from

God and was on track, following His will. But then I felt like it was all taken away.

I remember grieving the loss of this dream and once again being so angry at God. (Are you starting to see the kind of relationship we have?) I even begged my mom to let me lead the women's ministry from Houston, promising her I'd commute. I told her all the ways we would make it work. We both knew it wasn't going to happen, but I still tried.

In the meantime, I continued going to the women's team meetings every Tuesday. They continued to give me a voice, even though they knew I was moving. I would leave the meetings and just cry. I had no idea what God was doing or why, but I felt like I was supposed to keep showing up. So I did.

Then one day I was on the phone with a mentor, and I was processing *everything*. I honestly didn't understand what God could be up to. I felt so confused and heartbroken. After listening, she paused and said, "Hey, have you ever thought about how many women are in Houston?" And I stubbornly responded, "No. I don't really care! I like the women here in Dallas." She continued, "Well, I was just thinking how many women are in Houston. You've had prophetic words spoken about you minister-ing to large groups of women. Do you think it's possible that God would take you to Houston to reach the women there?"

> **An encounter with God through someone else changed everything for me!**

I suddenly felt like someone lifted my head out of my pain and frustration, and I could finally see. Like Hannah in the Bible, an encounter with God through someone else changed everything for me! Every word I had received over the years about women's ministry, I had tightly tied to the Dallas area and carrying on my mom's legacy. But God had something different in mind. I thought I would be someone who *carried on* something. I never thought God was calling me to carry it to another city and *build* there.

In hindsight, I'm so glad I kept showing up during that season because that time was invaluable. Through my tears and frustration, I continued to grow and learn how to do the role I desperately wanted, but God used it all for the role He had planned. Gateway Houston now has a thriving women's ministry, where I get to carry my mom's mantle in my voice, and it has been an honor and a joy to serve the women there.

In seasons of grief and change, the greatest lesson I've learned is to keep showing up. Be consistent in your good habits. Keep opening your Bible. Keep having your worship time. Keep praying. Keep pressing in. And if you need other resources, get them. Whether it's counseling, a new devotional or book, or a different version of the Bible to read. Just keep showing up. Even if you don't feel like it, even if you don't see immediate results or change, even if you think it's not relevant anymore. Keep showing up! It will do more than you realize. Our feelings and limited human outlook should not determine our commitment to our faith.

In the times when I stubbornly kept showing up, I can now look back and see so much fruit. Ethan always says there are some things that can only be produced through perseverance (see Romans 5:3–4), and I can affirm that's true. The valuable lessons I've learned in the waiting, in the persevering, in the showing up, I couldn't have learned anywhere else.

If you're in the midst of a dry or confusing season, if you're grieving a dream, if you're not sure what God is doing in your life today, I want to urge you to *keep showing up*. You won't be disappointed, dear friend. God doesn't waste a moment.

Finding Beauty in the Mess

What are you going to do to continue showing up this week? Is there an area of your life that God is redirecting?

A NEW VIEW

Debbie Morris

Do all that you can to live in peace with everyone.

Romans 12:18 (NLT)

A few years ago, I had an encounter with a lady who verbally attacked me. She said horrible and hateful things about Robert and me. I didn't know who she was, and I didn't know how to handle it. And the feelings I had from the encounter lingered with me for a long time.

A few weeks after the incident, I was interviewing a wonderful young girl for a position within our women's ministry. The interview was more of a formality because I had observed this incredible woman and knew I wanted her on my team. The interview was going really well until she made an innocent comment that triggered the memories of the awful encounter I had a few weeks earlier. When she made the comment, I stopped seeing her for who she truly was. Instead, I saw the other woman, and I reacted poorly.

The interview quickly went south. I made the job sound like the worst job in the world! I tried to convince myself I was simply underselling the role so that when she got into it, she'd be happy with how good it actually was. When we offered her the job, it was no surprise that she didn't take it. And I knew it was my fault.

The situation really bothered me. I had allowed a negative encounter to dictate how I reacted to someone else. It took me longer than it should have to call her and apologize. But I knew I had to remedy my mistake and fix this conflict by reaching out and asking for forgiveness. I couldn't fix the encounter I had with that first woman; however, I could repent and try to redeem my relationship with this sweet girl. Thankfully, she was understanding and graciously forgave me. She didn't accept the offer to work with me, although she did take another role within the church, and she's done an incredible job! Sometimes, when I see her in the halls or hear her name, I have a tinge of regret that I didn't get to work with her more closely, but I'm so thankful we're friends.

My behavior during that interview was one of a thousand mistakes

> People often want to avoid facing conflict or their own mistakes, but sometimes looking at them straight on is the only way to move forward.

I've made over the years, in ministry and at home. Yet I'm learning to own them and when necessary, to pick up the phone and have a conversation to make things right, no matter how difficult it may be. People often want to avoid facing conflict or their own mistakes, but sometimes looking at them straight on is the only way to move forward. Elaine says it this way: you can't heal what you're unwilling to acknowledge or pursue.

The Bible says to do all we can to live in peace with everyone. That might mean taking a good hard look at how you view other people. This might feel uncomfortable, but it's necessary. Maybe you need to pursue healing from difficult encounters or situations in your life. Maybe you need to pick up the phone or send an email or let go of a preconceived stereotype. Whatever it is, let the Holy Spirit guide you in this process.

First Samuel 16:7 says, "For the LORD does not see as man sees; for man looks at the outward appearance, but the LORD looks at the heart." God sees people for who they are, not what they do or how they look. And if we claim to be Christ followers, we need to do the same.

Our world is full of so much division and contempt, and when we acknowledge conflict and pursue healing, we take important steps toward the biblical, supernatural unity God desires for us (see Psalm 133:1). We are witnesses of God's great love to humanity, and we should lead the way. Can you imagine what the world would look like if we did that?

Finding Beauty in the Mess

Do you need to pursue healing from a difficult encounter? Or maybe there's someone you need to look at with a new view. Maybe there's someone you need to reach out to and ask for forgiveness. Take some time today to ask the Holy Spirit to guide you in this process.

I'M TAKING A NAP!

Elaine Fisher

Then Jesus said, "Come to me, all of you who are weary and carry heavy burdens, and I will give you rest."

Matthew 11:28 (NLT)

Every so often, I'm invited onto a Christian television show to talk about life and encourage people. It's always a great time, and I enjoy getting the chance to be a part.

On one show, we started to discuss what our quiet times looked like. One by one, the ladies took turns sharing about their quiet times. They would say something like, "Oh, I worship for an hour and then read the Bible for an hour." Each person had similar responses, and I started to panic about what I would say when it got to me.

I was the only one on the panel who had young children at home. My quiet times lately weren't exactly "quiet," and I never had much "time." Mickey Mouse Clubhouse was the background music to my Bible reading, and I had to finish reading before the last note played. When it was my turn to share, everyone looked at me, and I thought, *I guess I'll just tell the truth and see what happens!* I looked around the room and said, "If I have an hour to myself, I'm taking a nap!" We all laughed, and apparently, that was the right thing to say because they keep inviting me back!

Life is busy. It's demanding. Every season is different, but there are always things waiting to creep in and steal your time. Children need you. Work needs you. Your marriage needs you. Your friends need you. Everyone and everything is asking for your time. Sure, there are ways we could simplify life and lessen stress, but sometimes even that feels like just another to-do on the list. If you're like me, you may just be proud you found the time to read the words right in front of you. I get you.

And let's be real, sometimes taking a nap is holy.

You may have heard this story before, but I think it's worth repeating. There's an account in 1 Kings 19, where Elijah is being hunted by the evil queen Jezebel, and he flees into the wilderness. He's exhausted and he's afraid—he's just done. (I'm going to guess some of us have had days like this!) So Elijah prays a really depressing prayer and then falls asleep under a tree. An angel later awakens him, tells him

> **Sometimes taking a nap is holy.**

to eat some bread and drink some water that miraculously show up next to him, and then he falls asleep again. The angel wakes Elijah later and tells him to eat once more so he'll have strength for the journey ahead. Elijah does and then decides he's okay and continues in his journey.

Yes, the Lord could have given Elijah super-strength and energy to continue along in his journey without resting or eating. But He didn't. He let Elijah rest, not just for his physical health but for his mental health as well. Not only that, God provided for him in his place of rest. And He didn't get mad at Elijah for reaching a place of desperation and exhaustion. God simply met him right there in that place.

Maybe you find yourself in a desperate or exhausted place like Elijah today. Did you know that Jesus can relate? Even Jesus took moments in the crucial times of His ministry days to pull away and rest.

You don't have to feel bad about taking a nap. Rest is essential. And you don't have to have a picture-perfect quiet time either. God's desire is for you to connect with Him. So maybe, you have a moment with Him in the car while you're driving your kids to activities or washing the dishes. Maybe your prayer is that the Lord would speak to you in your dreams as you doze off while the kids nap.

Listen, God is there in all the in-between and messy moments of our lives. So don't let the enemy tell you that you are missing Him or not doing this Christian life right. Instead, be present with Him in the middle, and you will find that He will meet you in your place of desperation or exhaustion. There is grace for your season and even time for you to take a nap!

Finding Beauty in the Mess

Are you desperate or tired? Ask the Lord to meet you right where you are and give you rest.

RELATIONSHIP, NOT RELIGION

Debbie Morris

But be doers of the word,
and not hearers only, deceiving yourselves.

James 1:22

I may not read my Bible *every* day. I hesitate to broadcast this because I'm a pastor's wife, and my husband always tells people to read their Bible every day. But before you jump to conclusions, please hear me out.

I was talking about a certain verse recently, and someone asked me if I was reading through the Bible with a reading plan or if I happened upon that passage randomly. I responded, "I don't know. I'm not real consistent." Elaine jumped in for me and said, "No, Mom, you may not be consistent on *when* you read your Bible, but you're consistent in *how* you read your Bible."

I used to be very religious (for lack of a better word) about reading my Bible. I've been a Christian since I was a young girl, but I realized as I got older that at some point, I was only reading it every day to check it off my list or make myself feel like the good pastor's wife.

Then, a few years ago, I got into a rhythm of reading a passage or a story and just sitting with it for a couple of days. Now, I find a nugget of truth or something that jumps out at me, and I marinate on it. I pray about it throughout my day—while doing the dishes or running errands. I might break it down or study it. Then I ask God about it. What does He want me to learn or know from this passage? How can I live it out? Once I've thought and prayed about the passage for a bit, I'll read something else and think on that for a few days. I still sit with the Lord and commune with Him every day. But this way of experiencing God's Word has become so sweet for me.

In no way have I abandoned the Word; I've just abandoned the religious need to check it off my list every day. I want the *relationship*, not the religion.

I liken it to my marriage. Robert and I talk every day. We laugh, we eat together, and yes, we make love.

> We don't gain anything by checking off items on our good girl list. We only gain when we are transformed into God's likeness.

(Sorry, Elaine!) But it's when the moment is right. We don't usually plan it out. "Okay, on Thursdays at 7 pm, we will laugh for five minutes, and then we will make love. Check!" Sometimes the most pure, meaningful, and fun things happen out of relationship and time well spent together.

Let me be clear, God's Word is essential. Through His Word, He inscribes in us His heart and His ways. And while I may not read His words on a page daily, I am always thinking about God's Word. Let me explain. I know gossiping is wrong (see Proverbs 11:13). So after a lunch with girlfriends, I evaluate if I honored God with my words. Sometimes I have to repent, and then there are times when I think if there were a gossiping cliff, I was teetering on the edge of that deep chasm. Sometimes I have to ask myself if I helped younger women to love their husbands better by my example (see Titus 2:3–5). Recently, I've had to challenge myself to rejoice in difficulties (see James 1:2).

I have known scholars who can tell you nuances of Scripture but somehow miss that God is love. I don't want to be like that. We don't gain anything by checking off items on our good girl list. We only gain when we are transformed into God's likeness.

I think sometimes in an effort to disciple people, we can create robots instead of real people interested in a legitimate relationship with God. Certain personalities are driven by achievement or habit or perception, and if we're not careful, we can find ourselves going through the motions instead of growing. The Bible says we should not just hear the Word but do what it says (see James 1:22). But how can we do what it says when we don't take the time to fully process what it means? We need to take time to let the Word sink into our souls.

I don't want to read my Bible just to check it off my list for the day. I desire to give God's Word more space and reverence than that. I want to understand it and do what it says. I want to have an encounter with God through His Word. I'm not interested in being religious. I'm interested in being in relationship.

Finding Beauty in the Mess

Have you gotten into the habit of reading your Bible just to check it off your "to-do" list? How can you experience a more authentic relationship with God through His Word?

CHECK YOUR HEART

Elaine Fisher

You say, "I am allowed to do anything"—but not everything is good for you. You say, "I am allowed to do anything"— but not everything is beneficial.

1 Corinthians 10:23 (NLT)

*Y*ou know how different medications, lifestyles, and foods affect people in different ways? One person can have a cup of coffee at 10 pm and be happily asleep by 11 pm. But another person drinks a coffee at 3 pm and is wide awake until two in the morning. One person might be an early riser, and the other a night owl (and they marry each other). One person eats dairy and has no problems, while another has all sorts of unmentionable side effects—I'll stop there! We often acknowledge these differences in the physical sense but not as much in the mental or spiritual.

I've mentioned several times in this book the nature of my past—the promiscuity and partying and lying and giving in to peer pressure. As an adult, I have made adjustments in my life to protect my heart and mind. For instance, I am very intentional about what I watch, listen to, and even read. I know I can be easily influenced, and I want to guard myself from specific things. But my husband is not as easily influenced, nor does he have the past experiences I do. Ethan can watch a show and examine the characters' motivations and thought processes and then write a sermon about it! His mind is set, and he loves to learn about how other people think so he can be a better friend and pastor. God made us different from each other, and our experiences allow us to process things mentally, emotionally, and spiritually in unique ways. We all have different thermometers we use to gauge what we take in. Cutting out certain things in my life has made a huge difference in my daily walk with the Lord. And I wish I had learned this earlier in my life.

Having this personal awareness is so important, and I've started to teach my children about it, specifically my oldest daughter, Adde. In our family, the language we use with TV shows is that no show is "off-limits," although we obviously have a few we say we're choosing not to watch. But if

> I put everything I hear and see through this lens: is it constructive to my character and edifying to my spiritual life?

Adde turns on a show and is influenced by it in a way we feel doesn't honor God or the people around her, we stop allowing her to watch the show. This doesn't mean it's a terrible show; it simply means we see it influences her in a negative way. While we've had this conversation with her, sometimes she'll still ask, "Why can they watch that show and I can't?" We explain that how she perceives the show and how others perceive the show is different. How she takes in the information and how it affects her attitude and thought processes might not be honoring or good, but someone else may not respond to the show in the same way. Everyone's heart thermometer is sensitive to different things.

Let me just add that I do believe there are things Christ-followers should not let their eyes see and ears hear no matter what. There are some TV shows, movies, and even books that will impact *all* of us in negative ways, whether we choose to acknowledge it or not. But I'm specifically referring to sensitivity to general, age-appropriate media.

I'm so proud of Adde because she's learning to say, "This influences me in a different way, so I choose not to watch it." She's actually turned off shows and said, "I can tell I don't act the same after watching that show." My prayer is that as she gets older and as she is exposed to the wide range of media her generation has to offer, that she will continue to lean in to this sensitivity and protect her mind and spirit.

I like what the Amplified Bible Classic Edition translation of 1 Corinthians 10:23 says: "All things are legitimate [permissible—and we are free to do anything we please], but not all things are helpful (expedient, profitable, and wholesome). All things are legitimate, but not all things are constructive [to character] and edifying [to spiritual life]." I put everything I hear and see through this lens: is it constructive to my character and edifying to my spiritual life? It doesn't matter if my husband or best friend can watch a certain show, follow a certain social media account, or read a certain book. If it's not good for my mind and heart, I resist, and I'm always grateful I do.

Today, I encourage you to lean in to the Holy Spirit and check your heart thermometer. Then, if you feel something needs to be changed, do it. I promise you, it's well worth it.

Finding Beauty in the Mess

What is your heart thermometer saying to you today?
What are you sensitive to that others may not be?
Is it something you need to cut out of your life?

IN THE WEEDS

Debbie Morris

He was despised and rejected—a man of sorrows,
acquainted with deepest grief.

Isaiah 53:3 (NLT)

Six weeks after my dad was suddenly killed in a horrible tractor accident, we held our annual women's conference at Gateway Church. I came home from his memorial service and immediately had a conference to plan and execute. I didn't have a huge team helping me at that time. In fact, you might not even call it a team—it was just me and one other person—and putting on this conference required *a lot* from us.

I didn't realize it at the time, but all that planning gave me something to put my focus on and energy toward while I also grieved the death of my dad. My hands might have been busy, but my mind and heart were processing. After the conference ended, I continued to mourn, but it was different than I expected. And over the years I've discovered that grief can sometimes look different for each person and in each situation.

I'm not the poster child for grieving well, but as someone who has endured different kinds of losses over the years, I can share from my experiences. I've learned that when I'm processing something intense or grieving a loss—however big or small—I go into work mode. I busy myself in the garden, picking weeds and planting flowers. I clean out closets. I organize the garage. These aren't regular go-to activities for me. I'm not inclined to clean things out and organize on a daily basis, but I've discovered that when I need to work through some type of grief or sadness, finding something that needs to be done and putting my hands to it helps me process my feelings better.

Before I understood what I was doing or why, Robert would encourage me to stop working and sit down and rest. Without giving it a second thought, I would respond with, "I can't! The flowerbeds have weeds!" and quickly head back outside to tend my garden. But now Robert and the kids have recognized my pattern. My hands just need to do something

> I may not understand the depth of your loss or how you should handle it, but I know Someone who does.

easy and mundane while my mind and heart process. I work, work, work, praying all the while, until somewhere along the way I find a sense of peace. It's become how I pray through, process, and accept things. Elaine says when she sees me really busy doing stuff around the house and mumbling under my breath, she knows I'm working through something with the Lord and to give me some space.

While I wish that none of us had to endure any type of grief, I know it's inevitable. It's part of life. My guess is that many of you reading right now are working through some type of loss—whether it's a job, your health, a relationship, a marriage, a dream, or the death of a loved one. I may not understand the depth of your loss or how you should handle it, but I know Someone who does.

Isaiah 53:3 foretells that Jesus would be "a Man of sorrows, acquainted with grief." And He was. Jesus dwelled among us as a human for thirty-three years, and He encountered death and loss and disappointment and grief just like the rest of us. Scholars say that Jesus' earthly father, Joseph, died at some point in Jesus' teens or twenties. Jesus no doubt mourned that loss with His mother and siblings. And when Jesus' friend Lazarus died, He was moved with deep compassion for Mary and Martha and wept, too. Hebrews 4:14–16 says that Jesus, our High Priest, understands us because He faced all the same things we do. You may feel alone in your grief today, but Jesus understands. The Bible says He "care[s] about the anguish of [our] soul" (Psalm 31:7 NLT) and that God promises to be "close to the brokenhearted" (Psalm 34:18 NLT).

Grieving for you might look like scheduling a time to cry each day or breaking down at the grocery store while looking at tomatoes or going on a trip to remember your loved one or talking to a counselor or pastor. Or it might look like all these things! What I want you to know today is that Jesus does not leave you alone in your sadness and grief. He sits with you in it and offers you real hope for your future. Someday, "He will wipe every tear from their eyes, and there will be no more death or sorrow or crying or pain. All these things are gone forever" (Revelation 21:4 NLT). And I know that until that day comes, while I'm pulling weeds in my flowerbed, Jesus is right there with me, gloves in hand.

Finding Beauty in the Mess

Ask the Lord to meet you face to face and speak to you about your grief and how to walk through this season.
Don't be afraid or ashamed to talk to a counselor or pastor if you need to as well.

TUBING THROUGH LIFE

Elaine Fisher

For the word of God is living and powerful, and sharper than
any two-edged sword, piercing even to the division of soul and spirit,
and of joints and marrow, and is a discerner of the thoughts
and intents of the heart.

Hebrews 4:12

Over the years, I've seen fear start to become a big thing in my daughter Adde's life. So we discuss it a lot. I remind her that if we're not careful, fear will win. It will steal our joy. And then we talk about how to overcome it.

When Adde was really young, we went to the lake for our annual family vacation. We were having a great time out on the boat and decided to let her try tubing. We attached the ski tube to the back of the boat with a rope and carefully put her on the tube. We showed her how to hold on and explained everything that was going to happen. We also made sure to tell her how much fun it was going to be!

Once we got Adde settled and she felt ready to go, we pushed her out behind the boat and started slowly moving. As I watched her, I expected to see her laughing or a least a big smile. Instead, she looked tense and shaky, and although I couldn't hear her voice over the roar of the boat engine, I saw her mouth moving. I thought, *What is going on?!*

After a few minutes, we pulled her in, and I asked, "Adde, what were you saying?" She responded, "I was *so* scared! So I started saying, 'For God has not given me a spirit of fear, but of power, love, and a sound mind.' And I said it over and over and over again."

I was so proud of her! And I was so grateful we gave her *truth* to declare over herself. It wasn't a cliché or an opinion or a popular phrase that she found courage in. It wasn't just something Ethan or I said to her a lot. It was the Word of God in her mouth! The living and active Word of God. Hebrews 4:12 says that the Word of God is "sharper than any two-edged sword." It can cut through anything with precision,

> **God's Word has an answer for everything we may encounter in this life, big or small. It equips us to navigate and conquer every situation.**

even an overwhelming fear of tubing. Tubing may not be a scary thing to you, but it was a big deal for my Adde. And she tackled her fear with God's Word!

I want to ask you a question: What do you say to yourself when you're scared or confused or struggling? Is it a motivational phrase? Does a curse word slip out? Is it a self-deprecating comment about your own abilities or personality? I don't want to introduce shame to you if your answer is less than holy. And having a personal motto or phrase isn't bad. But I challenge you today to make the *Word of God* the ultimate truth you repeat and hold onto while tubing through life.

God's Word has an answer for everything we may encounter in this life, big or small. It equips us to navigate and conquer *every* situation. It's timeless, and its pages hold wisdom and strength and power for our generation and for generations to come. I often pray for my kids to get something beyond the limited knowledge Ethan and I can share with them, and I know the only thing that will truly make a lasting difference in their lives is the Word of God.

Let's make a commitment today not only to memorize or repeat the Word of God but also to let it go deep into our souls, changing us from the inside out. There are several times in the Bible where Jesus rebukes those who had memorized a lot of Scripture but didn't know how to let it change their lives and hearts (see Matthew 23:1–25). There are many Christians out there who know how to talk the talk. They know the words to say and how to act in front of others, but their hearts are not abiding in Jesus. (I know this because I did this during my teenage years!) If that sounds like you too, remember it's never too late to come to Jesus in repentance.

When you read the Word today, I encourage you to let it seep into your heart and mind. Mediate on what it means and how to apply it to your life. And the next time you go tubing, even if no one can hear you, speak it out!

Finding Beauty in the Mess

Ask the Holy Spirit to give you His Word for every situation you encounter and to hide it deep in your heart.

IN THE VINE

Debbie Morris

"I am the vine, you are the branches. He who abides in Me,
and I in him, bears much fruit; for without Me you can do nothing."

John 15:5

One of our most memorable vacations was when we spent a week at the beach in Florida with our three grown kids, their spouses, and all our grandkids. When we finally arrived at the beautiful beach house we rented, we discovered the upstairs air conditioning had gone out, and it couldn't be fixed until our last day. Those of us in downstairs rooms slept fine (although Josh and Hannah were sleeping in bunk beds), but James and Bridgette's room was upstairs. As you can guess, they didn't sleep great. I don't know about you, but a Florida summer night without air conditioning or sleeping in a kid's bunk bed would be enough to make me cranky!

Then one day we decided to go deep sea fishing, and Elaine got really seasick. (Actually, it was probably more morning sickness than motion sickness. She was carrying a secret—her name is Kate.) She was throwing up over the side of the boat nearly the whole time. Ethan was trying to take care of her, but then he got queasy too. Ethan and Elaine insisted the family keep on fishing, so we did, and the boys caught a lot of fish and had a great time. (Robert says it was because Elaine was providing great bait! I know, gross!)

That trip had some rough moments! There were reasons for our kids to complain and be unhappy, yet no one griped or complained all week. Robert and I were so proud of them!

That trip revealed to us that our kids and their spouses grew up and were producing good fruit. They all displayed kindness and patience and self-control. We could tell by their fruit that they were abiding in the Vine. Jesus said in John 15:5, "I am the vine, you are the branches." And on that trip we could see from their actions how passionately our kids were abiding in Jesus. Through their surrendered hearts, the Holy Spirit gave our kids the love, joy, peace, patience, kindness, goodness, faithfulness, gentleness, and self-control to get through that trip!

That's not to say our kids never complain—they do! And if they had complained, we wouldn't have said, "Nope! No fruit of the Spirit for them!" But it was good for our parent hearts to

> **We could tell by their fruit that they were abiding in the Vine.**

experience that moment. We all could have complained our way through that trip. It could have made for a bad memory. But because of the good fruit in their lives, this trip remains a sweet memory for us.

You may be having a rough week, a rough month, or even a rough year. Your kids or your coworkers may be driving you over the edge. Joy may be a really difficult thing right now. Peace may seem like a dream. We've all had those moments when you just want to scream. But when you abide in the Vine, when you stick close to Jesus *every day*, the Holy Spirit will give you supernatural love, joy, peace, patience, kindness, goodness, faithfulness, gentleness, and self-control to get through.

Some of the fruits may come easily to you, while others may be more of a stretch, but the fruit of the Spirit doesn't just happen. It's through intentional abiding. And I promise that, as you remain connected with Christ, He will give you what you need to endure well. And in the moments when the lack of air conditioning gets to you, He is there to gently convict your heart and give you grace for the next thing.

And you never know who might be watching. When the Holy Spirit empowers you to display good fruit wherever you are, whatever your circumstances, someone else will see Jesus through you!

Finding Beauty in the Mess

*Do you think your life produces the fruit of the Spirit? Would
the people around you say the same?
Ask the Holy Spirit to empower you to abide in Him
so you can display good fruit in every circumstance.*

THE BEST LIFE

Elaine Fisher

*Death and life are in the power of the tongue,
and those who love it will eat its fruit.*

Proverbs 18:21

Recently, someone gave me a T-shirt that says, "Mom Life Is the Best Life." I love it and wear it often. One Saturday, I was wearing it while running errands and doing chores around the house. Later that night, I was helping Adde with something, and she suddenly stopped, looked at me, and said, "Mom, is 'mom life' really the best life?"

Most days I *love* being a mom—it's the life I wished for since I was five years old. My kids are the answers to many of my prayers, and I wouldn't trade them for anything. However, there are days that are more difficult or heavy or days when I'm tired, and it doesn't feel like it's the best life. This was one of *those* days. And without thinking, I replied to Adde, "Some days."

I regretted my response and thought about it for days. Have you ever wanted to rewind time and take back your words? Even when I'm weary or unsure, I don't want to be so quick to spout off words that may put doubt or fear into my kids. I don't want to create negative impressions about me, our family, or their future families in their minds because of my lack of confidence or exhaustion. I want them to know when they grow up and move out of the house and have their own families that their dad and I really loved them and our lives together.

This moment made me realize that my kids are watching everything! They watch the things I do, they see the words on my clothing, and they really listen to the words that come out of my mouth.

But I don't think this is only about my kids. No matter who you are—whether you're a parent, businessperson, pastor, teacher, plumber, or college student—someone is watching how you live your life and listening to the words you speak. What will they hear? What will they learn? We all have an area of influence, and the things we say matter. That doesn't mean we can't live authentically or be honest about how we feel. But we need to remember that we have the power of life

> **We all have an area of influence, and the things we say matter.**

and death in our tongues (see Proverbs 18:21). Our words can do great damage or bring miraculous healing.

The Bible says in Ephesians 4:29 (ESV), "Let no corrupting talk come out of your mouths, but only such as is good for building up, as fits the occasion, that it may give grace to those who hear." Now, the words I said to Adde were not the worst words I've ever said, by any means. Nor were they corrupt. They were maybe honest in that moment, but without clarification, they weren't edifying, and they didn't give grace to my daughter. (This is another reason I'm so grateful for the grace God gives when I mess up!)

The Lord has been teaching me lately to be more intentional with how I communicate and portray my life, especially on days when I'm cranky or tired. It's not about putting on rose-colored glasses and pretending life is hunky-dory when it's not. It's about being slow to speak and considering the implications of the words I say. It's about looking for the blessings in the middle of the mess. I've been challenging myself in this, and I want to encourage you as well. You can bring blessing and peace and grace and love and joy with the words you say. Your words can bring people closer to Jesus and His truth. Your words can bring life.

If I were to have a do-over with Adde that day, I think I'd say, "Some days are tough, but I love our family more than anything. Mom life *truly* is the best life."

Finding Beauty in the Mess

*What kind of words do you typically speak over
yourself or your family?
What life-giving words can you say instead?*

POOP ON THE STAIRS

Elaine Fisher

This is the day the LORD has made;
we will rejoice and be glad in it.

Psalm 118:24

I had my four kids pretty close together in age, so there was a good five-year stint of my life that felt like we used a bajillion diapers a day. I honestly thought it would never end, and I wanted *out* of the diaper phase. I thought about it. I dreamed about it. I prayed for it. And I celebrated hard when each one graduated to the potty.

But I'll never forget the day my third child, Preston, was upstairs and decided to take off his poopy diaper and very carefully slide his sweet little butt down the carpeted stairs (just like we'd taught him), all the way into the living room.

Poop was everywhere. I mean *everywhere*!

My first reaction was to just lie down and cry. Hours of cleaning were ahead, and it felt overwhelming. But something in me said, "Choose laughter." Perhaps it was growing up hearing stories about eating pie off the floor. Or maybe it was some sort of manic response to keep me from crying. Whatever the reason, I chose to laugh. It was a little forced at first, but eventually it came naturally and made the day better. Instead of crawling back into bed and dreaming about a diaper-free future, I cleaned up my son, gave him a hug, deep cleaned the carpet on my stairs and in my living room, and sold my house. (We really did sell the house a few months later, although for reasons unrelated to poopy stairs.)

Looking back, I would love to have another day in diaper season. I realize now there were days I didn't fully embrace or enjoy the time at home with my littles. Days when I was tired and overwhelmed. Days when I wasn't so sure my T-shirt that says, "Mom Life Is the Best Life" really rang true. I kept looking ahead to the next season, the next checkpoint, the next bit of freedom, instead of being present in the everyday moments.

> **Don't miss the blessing of the season you're in because you're looking for the next one.**

Recently, I was helping Adde wash her hair. As she was rinsing out the shampoo, I grabbed my phone to look at something, and I heard the Lord say, "Put down your phone." Not sure what else to do with myself while waiting for her, I decided to ask Adde if there was anything she wanted to talk to me about. She started opening up and sharing with me about how she saw someone make a gesture at school and didn't know what it meant. Her friends had made fun of her because she didn't know what it was, and it had been weighing heavily on her. Although I realized I would rather have been cleaning poop off the stairs than talking about all the things she's being exposed to at school, I was happy to have this moment with her and speak life and truth to her. I didn't want to rush past it or miss it. I knew one day I'd look back and be thrilled that I put my phone down and fully embraced this moment together.

While we numbly stare at our phones, the world passes us by. While we focus solely on the hardships we're navigating, the good things right in front of us go unnoticed. While we worry about the future, our present wastes away. If we're not careful, days and seasons might pass us by without so much of a blink. Or to quote the wise words of Ferris Bueller: "Life moves pretty fast. If you don't stop and look around once in a while, you could miss it."

The Bible says to rejoice in each day the Lord has made (see Psalm 118:24) and not to worry about tomorrow (see Matthew 6:34). Don't miss the blessing of the season you're in because you're looking for the next one. I have wasted precious time praying for the season that's next. When I was a stay-at-home mom, I was so worn out and thought being a working mom would be so much easier. Then, when I became a working mom, I kind of wanted to go back! But the Lord has been working in me, and I've learned to be grateful and to value the season I'm in *right now*.

I encourage you to lift up your head and open your eyes today. Look around. Each day is a blessing to cherish, even if there's poop on the stairs!

Finding Beauty in the Mess

How can you be mentally and emotionally available
for the people around you today?
Do you need to put down your phone?
Do you need to stop worrying about the future?
Ask the Holy Spirit to speak to you about where you are and
how to be fully present in it.

THE WELLSPRING OF LIFE

Debbie Morris

Finally, brethren, whatever things are true, whatever things are noble, whatever things are just, whatever things are pure, whatever things are lovely, whatever things are of good report, if there is any virtue and if there is anything praiseworthy —meditate on these things.

Philippians 4:8

*S*ometimes people ask me what my favorite Bible verse is, and I think they expect me to respond with a super common verse or one that's really inspirational. But the guiding Scripture in my life is actually a short little verse of caution hidden within Proverbs. It says, "Above all else, guard your heart, for everything you do flows from it"

(Proverbs 4:23 NIV). Other versions say, "Keep your heart with all diligence, for out of it is the wellspring of life" (WEB), and "Watch over your heart with all diligence, for from it flow the springs of life" (AMP). This verse doesn't feel particularly exciting like Jeremiah 29:11 or Romans 8:28 might, but it's special to me and one that guides my life.

What was the last thing you guarded? Was it the last brownie in the pan? Was it your eyes from the sun? Was it your home from a big storm? Was it your child from an oncoming car? What exactly does it mean to guard your heart?

Often in the Old Testament, the word "heart" is used to mean a person's thought life, emotions, or motivations. Our hearts are closely connected to our thoughts and emotions. For me, Proverbs 4:23 is a reminder to put up a shield between my mind and the enemy's schemes to cause division, destruction, and strife in my life. It reminds me that I have a choice when something happens that hurts or offends me. I can either guard my heart and mind from it, or I can think on it and think on it and think on it so much that the offense becomes much bigger than it actually is.

As a pastor's wife, I've had plenty of reason not to trust people or to be offended by people. Over the years people have said a lot of things about me and my family, and

> When I guard my heart from any perceived or actual wounds, I can move forward in peace and unity.

I've had to guard my heart and let it go; otherwise, I'd be swallowed up in bitterness. I've had people approach me to apologize for something, and I don't even know what they're apologizing for! They'll mention what they did or said, but I wouldn't have remembered it if they hadn't brought it up! I work so hard at guarding my heart and not ruminating on offenses that they simply disappear.

When I don't let little offenses build to bigger offenses in my heart, I'm healthier, my marriage is healthier, my relationships with my kids are healthier, my friendships are healthier. When life abundant springs from my heart, instead of anger or frustration, it's a much better way to live.

There is a battle for our hearts and minds every single day. The enemy wants to steal, kill, and destroy everything about your life—your friendships, your marriage, your family, your career. And he often starts with your heart and mind. But this verse reminds me that I don't have to let him. I can guard my heart and take every thought captive (see 2 Corinthians 10:5). It has taken years of practice, but I know when I guard my heart from any perceived or actual wounds, I can move forward in peace and unity. My heart is full of *life* and good things, not unforgiveness or anger. The Bible says to think on good, praiseworthy things (see Philippians 4:8), and when we do, there isn't room for the bad thoughts. Guard your heart today.

Finding Beauty in the Mess

*Do you need to guard your heart and mind from something? If you're struggling today with an offense,
whether it was intentional or a mistake, don't let it fester.
Ask the Holy Spirit to fill your heart and mind
with good things.*

SOFT HEART, THICK SKIN

Elaine Fisher

*And He said to me, "My grace is sufficient for you,
for My strength is made perfect in weakness."*

2 Corinthians 12:9

Since planting a church, I've started to experience some of the things my parents went through in ministry that I didn't quite understand as a kid. I didn't understand that real friendships were difficult to maintain. I didn't understand the pressure that comes with leading. I didn't understand how hard it was to have people come in and out of your life, to have people walk out or betray you or do things to compromise your trust. I didn't understand that people could love you and hate you in the same sentence.

Yet, I watched my mom and dad navigate these situations with grace and love.

My mom especially taught me how to live this out. I've never met somebody with so much grace. She always says, "Let's just extend grace." I remember praying to be like my mom, so it was such a gift when I got a prophetic word that said, "You have your mom in you!" She is so good at continuing to love people, despite the ways people have treated her in the past.

But I have to admit, the first time some of these things happened to me, it *really* hurt. I remember asking the Lord, "How can I have a soft heart toward people but thick skin?" I didn't want to lose my soft heart because I believe God uses soft hearts to reach hurting people, but I also didn't want to walk around wounded and broken. I didn't want to shutter my heart away or be jaded and cynical toward people. I needed some thick skin—a soft heart but thick skin.

I know I'm not the only one who might need this. There is so much division and upset in the world today—people are openly criticizing each other's political views, religious views, and even diet choices. It can be so easy to close off our hearts to others in an effort to protect ourselves from hurt. That's what the enemy wants because it stops us from loving and caring for people.

> When we keep our hearts soft and see people through the eyes of Jesus, miracles happen.

But that's not what the Bible teaches us about loving people (see Mark 12:30–31).

There's a passage in the first chapter of Jeremiah the Lord has used to wreck my heart on multiple occasions. I have so much to say about this passage (I've preached entire messages on it!), but I specifically want to look at what God says in verses 11 and 13. He asks Jeremiah, "What do you see?" Jeremiah responds with what he sees, and God basically says, "Good, and here's what it means." God was entrusting Jeremiah with nations and people, and He needed Jeremiah to see them like He did.

I think the secret to having a soft heart and thick skin is vision. We must ask the Lord to teach us how to see people through *His* eyes. We need to teach our children how to see people with *His* perspective. Jesus was often "moved with compassion" when He encountered people (see Matthew 14:14, 15:32, 20:32), and when we seek to see people through His eyes, we will be too, no matter what they do or how they may hurt us. You can develop grace for them. And you know what happened almost every time Jesus was moved with compassion for those around Him? *Miracles.* When we keep our hearts soft and see people through the eyes of Jesus, miracles happen.

Today, you can make the choice to love like Jesus. Ask Him to help you see people as He does. Let your heart be moved to compassion and grace for them. Let your heart break for their brokenness. But also guard your heart from any hurtful actions designed to divide. And when you don't think you have grace available, remember that God's grace is there for you and is sufficient in every circumstance. His power is made perfect in our weakness (see 2 Corinthians 12:9–10), and we can pull from His endless supply anytime.

Finding Beauty in the Mess

Who do you need to see through God's eyes?
Who do you need to extend grace to?

FROM MUNDANE TO MIRACULOUS

Debbie Morris

*Whatever you do, do it heartily, as to the Lord
and not to men, knowing that from the Lord you
will receive the reward of the inheritance;
for you serve the Lord Christ.*

Colossians 3:23–24

When I was leading our women's ministry, we were always planning the next conference or women's night. We prayed fervently for *every* detail of these events, but a majority of our time was spent coordinating the details—décor, contracts and travel for speakers, people to serve in worship and tech, and logistics for the event space. These things didn't feel very spiritual, but they were necessary. They were all practical tasks on our list of things to do. *What flight should the speaker take? What color scheme should we have for our décor? What games should we play? What snacks should we provide?*

And then, the miraculous would happen. Everything would come together (sometimes just hours beforehand), and God would move in the hearts and lives of the women.

It was always amazing! We would submit everything to God, and He would orchestrate every detail. For instance, many times at our larger events our speakers would share on the same topic, even though we provided no guidance. It was obvious God had something specific our women needed to hear! Or we would put together a fun playlist to play in the lobby, and the Lord would use a random song to speak exactly what someone needed to hear.

After more than twenty years of ministry, I've heard hundreds of testimonies of what God has done at our events—deaf women healed, broken relationships mended, finances miraculously provided, people called into ministry, babies conceived after years of infertility. The thing is, putting together the details of those events often felt mundane or frustrating or even silly. But I've found that even choosing what color balloons to get or flowers to buy

> **When we commit even the smallest, ordinary things to God, He will orchestrate the details into something miraculous!**

is important. When we commit even the smallest, ordinary things to God, He will orchestrate the details into something miraculous!

I love to paint, so I like to think of it like a painting. When I'm painting, my family and friends only see the whole picture once I'm done—they don't see each individual brush stroke. But every single paint stroke, no matter how small, is important to making the whole painting come to life.

Every moment of our lives, every task we perform, can all work together to build a life filled with God's presence and power. Susanna Wesley, the mother of theologian John Wesley, prayed, "Help me, Lord, to remember that religion is not to be confined to the church . . . nor exercised only in prayer and meditation, but that everywhere I am in Thy Presence." And Colossians 3:23-24 says, *"Whatever you do, do it heartily, as to the Lord and not to men, knowing that from the Lord you will receive the reward of the inheritance; for you serve the Lord Christ"* (emphasis added). You may have heard this verse. You may have even heard this message. But it's worth the reminder when you're up to your ears in diapers or paperwork or dishes and you're discouraged. God can use *anything* we've submitted to Him, even laundry, to become a moment to meet with Him or for Him to move in the people around you.

I don't know what you have on your plate today. Maybe it's driving your kids around or doing a mountain of laundry. Maybe it's inputting data at work or grocery shopping. We all have those mundane, ordinary, sometimes boring tasks to complete, but that doesn't mean they're not holy or spiritual. You never know how God will use something mundane to do something miraculous. I've seen it happen. I know you can too.

Finding Beauty in the Mess

What are the mundane and boring details of your life that you
wouldn't typically pray about or submit to the Lord?
Take a moment today to bring those things to the Lord,
and ask Him to meet you in the midst of them.
You'll become more aware of God's presence in the small,
ordinary moments when you submit them to Him.

IRREGULAR HEARTBEATS

Elaine Fisher

"A new command I give you: Love one another.
As I have loved you, so you must love one another."

John 13:34 (NIV)

*M*y son Preston loves school, but one week, he was adamant about not doing his homework, which wasn't normal for him. When he asked to be picked up early the next day, I immediately texted my husband and said, "We need to lean in." I made sure I was one of the first cars in the pick-up line, and that night I paid special attention to him and made his homework time fun. He was a different kid after that.

I don't know if he just had a weird couple of days or if something more was going on. While I could have just ignored it and thought, *His tummy just hurts or something. He's fine,* I knew this was irregular for him. So I cleared my schedule to make sure it wasn't something we needed to dive into more.

When situations like this happen with my family or with my team at church, I like to call them *irregular heartbeats—* the times when someone seems off, their behavior changes, or they stop doing something they normally do. In medical terms, an irregular heartbeat could be an indication that something is wrong, or it could be harmless. But an exam is recommended to make sure treatment isn't necessary. I have learned that when I see irregularities in someone's behavior, like an irregular heartbeat, it's worth looking into. And I believe there are two ways to handle it. We either communicate with the heart and demand it be regular again or we do tests to find out why it's beating irregularly.

I remember the day I stopped serving in children's ministry when I was a teenager. Before that, I had been so committed that even when my dad and I got into a motorcycle accident, I told the paramedics I needed to be at church by 3 pm to serve in the toddler classroom! I was *committed*! But when I was told I wasn't needed in that room anymore, instead of serving elsewhere, I

> Jesus tells us that the greatest commandment is to love God, and the second is to love others. Recognizing when someone's rhythm is off is love.

stopped serving altogether. It was a pivotal moment for me and led to a breakdown of other things in my life.

In hindsight, I can see that I felt like I didn't belong there anymore. I lost my sense of purpose and significance. But no one took the time to find that out, and no one asked me why I stopped serving. Even though I knew I was going off the rails, I never actually stopped to ask myself *how* I was doing or *why* I was making the choices I was making. And no one else asked me either. I'm not blaming anyone. I was a fantastic liar, and I wouldn't have told the truth anyway. But I've often wondered if things might have been different if someone had been intentional to ask about my irregular heartbeat.

This is why I am intentional with the people in my life, especially now that I'm raising little ones and leading teams at church. If I see something out of place or a regular rhythm of behavior being interrupted, you better believe I'm going to start asking questions: *How are you doing? How's your heart? What are you feeling? What is going on in your thought life?* It doesn't need to be a full-scale episode of *Intervention*, but these questions are how I love and care for the people around me.

I might not use this exact language with my younger kids, but I'm going to find a way to get their heartbeat on track again. And I will make myself available to process with them on why it went out of rhythm in the first place if needed. I understand that behavior and rhythms change as you grow, but I don't want to miss the chance to speak into those moments because I'm tired or have a deadline. If one of my kids is crying about wanting to quit a sport they were excited about, I'm not going to leave, even if I have somewhere else to be. I'm going to sit down and find out why. It's too important to me, so I make time, cancel plans, or arrive places late without any regrets.

Jesus tells us that the greatest commandment is to love God, and the second is to love others. Recognizing when someone's rhythm is off is love. But it's not just about recognizing their irregular heartbeats. It's not just saying, "Hey, So-and-So is acting really weird lately. Hmm." It's *doing something* that shows love and care like Jesus. The Bible says that faith without action is dead (see James 2:17), and the same applies to love. "My little children, let us not love in word or in tongue, but in deed and in truth" (1 John 3:18).

And because I never want to leave out an opportunity for self-reflection or an encounter with God, I'm asking you today: do *you* have an irregular heartbeat? Is there something that's off or not beating correctly? I encourage you to invite the Holy Spirit to speak to you and get your heart back on a rhythm with His heart.

Finding Beauty in the Mess

Is someone around you exhibiting an irregular heartbeat?
Have you investigated why?

THE EYE OF THE STORM

Debbie Morris

But immediately Jesus spoke to them, saying,
"Be of good cheer! It is I; do not be afraid."

Matthew 14:27

*P*ublic speaking doesn't come naturally to me. Anyone who knows me will tell you I don't enjoy being the center of attention or speaking in front of large groups of people. But the one time Robert convinced me to preach on a weekend at Gateway Church, I spoke about being at peace in the middle of a storm. I shared three points: There will be storms. There will be temptations in the storms. There will be benefits to the storms. I didn't know it at the time, but years later this message would not only be one I remembered but one I greatly needed.

In April 2018, Robert and I were at our ranch house. It's in a rural location, so we go out there often to rest and rejuvenate. Robert didn't feel well one morning, so while he slept in, I sat in bed with my phone. I opened the Bible app and happened upon the story of Lazarus in John 11. Jesus had just heard that His dear friend Lazarus was sick, and verse 5 says, "Now Jesus loved Martha and her sister and Lazarus." I read the rest of the story where Jesus resurrected Lazarus from the dead, but I kept thinking back on verse 5. I thought, *God, You* really *loved them.* And then I thought, *God, You* really *love Robert too!*

Later that day, Robert still wasn't feeling well and collapsed in the bathroom. I immediately called the paramedics, and they were able to revive him. But then a few hours later, he passed out a second time. The paramedics came again, but this time they couldn't find a pulse. Things didn't look good at all, so the paramedics called a helicopter to take him to the hospital. During all this, I had a flood of thoughts: *Lord, did I miss something You said this morning? Were you preparing me for something, and I wasn't listening?*

The helicopter lifted off with my dying husband inside, and I raced to the car to begin the long drive to the hospital on my own. I had my phone and Robert's phone with me, and I was getting calls and texts from the kids, but I ignored them because

> **It's within the storms that you get to see Jesus more clearly.**

I was contending in prayer for Robert's life and asking God to be merciful to our family. It was an intense drive, but I made it to the hospital in record time and spent the next few days there, desperately praying for God to save my husband's life. Even though he had another life-threatening scare while in the hospital, God was gracious, and He saved his life. God gets all the glory for miraculously healing Robert.

It's been several years since this crisis, but I still get asked how I felt during this time and if I ever questioned God's love. When I think back, I remember knowing that whatever happened, as horrible as it would be if Robert died, God would take care of my heart, and He would take care of our family. I rested in the fact that the Lord loved me, *and* He loved Robert. I had this unexplainable peace. The peace that passes all understanding really did meet me in my car (see Philippians 4:7). It was like I was in the eye of a storm, in perfect peace.

After experiencing Robert's health scare, I believe the three points I shared from the platform years earlier still stand. There have been storms in my life. More than just the one I shared here. There will be more, too. Jesus says that we *will* have trouble in this world (see John 16:33).

And the temptations during the storms have been real. On the drive to the hospital that day, I was tempted by fear. I won't deny, belittle, or gloss over the fact that fear is real. Robert was very close to death. But I chose to fight fear with faith and believe in God's love, goodness, and provision, no matter the outcome.

The last point is sometimes hard to believe when you're in the midst of the swirling waves and crushing wind. But it's within the storms that *you get to see Jesus more clearly.* In every crisis, every tough situation, every hospital visit, every tear that falls, Jesus is right there in the boat with us, and He offers us His peace. If we open our hearts to His presence, we can feel Him walking alongside us, guiding us to the other side. And we come out knowing Him better than before.

I don't know what kind of storms you may be facing in your life right now or what you will experience in the future. But there is an eye in every storm, and His name is Jesus. Lean into His presence, and hear Him say, "Peace, be still!" (Mark 4:39). Rest assured knowing He's there, and He loves you dearly.

Finding Beauty in the Mess

How can you continue to live with hope during a storm? Will
you rest in the fact that the Lord loves you and
will take care of you?
Will you receive His supernatural peace?

BE UNAPOLOGETICALLY YOU

Elaine Fisher

For You formed my inward parts;
You covered me in my mother's womb
I will praise You, for I am fearfully and wonderfully made.

Psalm 139:13

*G*od often gives me a word or phrase to focus on for different times in my life. Sometimes the words last for a short period, and other times they stick with me for a couple of years. Sometimes they come through my personal time with God, and other times they come through a mentor or friend. But the Lord has been pressing one particular phrase on my heart the past few years, and it's one that I know I will continue to hold on to.

Growing up, the temptation to try to be Robert Morris Jr. or Debbie Morris 2.0 was real. Everybody loves my parents, and they have impacted thousands of lives, including mine, so why wouldn't I want to be like them? As I've mentioned, I am easily influenced by people around me—I've been that way since I was a kid. So as an adult in ministry that manifested as, "Well, I love how Charlotte Gambill preaches, so I should preach like her." Or "I should be more like Joyce Meyer." Or "Dad would say it this way."

Then one day a mentor said to me: *be unapologetically you.* These words resonated so deeply that I knew they weren't just something catchy he was saying—they were from God for me. This set me on a journey to find out who *I* am and what *I* would say and how *I* would say it. God didn't create me to be a mini Priscilla Shirer or a Christine Caine 2.0. That's not to say I can't learn and grow from watching or emulating others who are experts or seasoned in their fields. There's definitely merit in that. But this phrase propelled me to find my voice and settle into who God has called me to be, not who I think I should be.

I began asking myself questions: *Do I know with clarity what God has called me to do? Or will I get distracted doing the next big thing? Am I going to get distracted because everybody else is*

> **The only Person we need to seek to be like is Jesus.**

preaching about this? Am I going to get distracted by how that mom does things? Will I be confident in who God has called me to be? Will I do everything He says to me?

Listen, don't waste your life chasing after who you *think* you should be or even who someone else thinks you should be. You may miss out on who you could be—who you were created to be! We often live in "shoulds," and it can hinder us from becoming who we're meant to be in Christ. God created you to be *you*. God did not call you to be someone else. He already has them. And He will not anoint a mask. He called you to be *you* because He needs *your* voice in this day and age. What would have happened if Esther had decided she needed to be more like Ruth? Or if Mary decided she should be like Martha?

Who are you trying to be? Is it a parent, a relative, a pastor, someone on social media, a friend, or a famous person? We can respect people and admire the qualities they have, but *the only Person we need to seek to be like is Jesus.* Second Corinthians 3:18 says that when we see God for who and what He truly is, we can be transformed into His image through the Holy Spirit. Look to Jesus. He is the only one worth mirroring. So go ahead and whip out those old WWJD bracelets!

Today, I want you to release the limits on who you are. I want you to release the pressure you have placed on yourself. You have a unique perspective, a unique experience, and a unique influence on your world that God created *you* to impact. And your voice might be the one to save a generation (see Esther 8. Well, actually, check out the whole book of Esther!).

God created you in His image. Stop looking for you in someone else. Be unapologetically *you*!

Finding Beauty in the Mess

Who are you tempted to emulate?
Ask the Lord today to show you how He sees you and
who He has called you to be.

OAKS OF RIGHTEOUSNESS

Debbie Morris

*In their righteousness, they will be like great oaks that
the LORD has planted for his own glory.*

Isaiah 61:3 (NLT)

When I was in my twenties, I had a yellow Volkswagen that we affectionately called The Yellow Submarine. One day as I was driving down a busy highway, it sprang a fuel leak. My gas tank went from full down to nothing in the middle of rush-hour traffic, leaving me stranded in the center median.

It wasn't long before a nice man came along and filled up my tank with gas. I offered to pay him, but he refused, and said, "No, you had this one coming!"

Thinking back, this small act of kindness reminded me so much of my dad. He had done this same type of thing for thousands of people over the years, and here I was seeing his legacy come to life.

I grew up in East Texas where my dad loved riding his tractor and working the land. He had a practical know-how born out of years of experience and hard work—there were things he did on our land that no one else knew how to do. He also had a mechanical gifting that I wish had transferred to me. He loved working with his hands and could fix just about anything.

He also used his gifts and talents to help people in our neighborhood and local community. Whether he was mowing someone's yard or doing car repairs for a family with special needs, he was always available and lending a hand.

My family and I didn't know the extent of his influence until he passed away. Over time, we kept hearing more and more stories about what he had done for others. He didn't preach from a pulpit, but he pastored people well, and his acts of kindness left a significant impact on the people in the community.

When I was a kid, he and I planted an oak tree. Oaks are tough trees with deep root systems that serve as anchors in hardships and tempests. The oak we planted all those years ago is huge now (which, honestly, makes me feel old), and you can still see it towering outside the house we

> **You may think the small things you do on a daily basis don't matter in the grand scheme of things, but they do.**

lived in when I was a kid. It required a lot of watering and fertilizing to make it grow tall and strong, but our hard work paid off, and now others get to enjoy its shade.

That old oak tree is a good representation of my family's legacy. You see, legacy isn't something that just happens. It's a culmination of small things that make it grow. Day in and day out, sun and water, roots grow deep, through wind and storms.

It was *years* of my dad being kind and generous and loving, day in and day out, toward the people around him that created the incredible legacy that my family has had the honor and privilege to build upon. It was *years* of him tithing regularly and teaching us to do the same. It was *years* of him stopping on the side of the road to help with someone's car, even if we were headed out on vacation or somewhere important. It was *years* of him serving others with the gifts the Lord had given him. And if he saw someone who needed something, he would try to give. He loved God, and he loved people.

Now, my kids, my grandkids, and I are all sitting under the shade of a tree we didn't plant. We enjoy the fruit from its branches and scatter even more of its good seeds. We are reaping all the good things he sowed. We are being reciprocated in good measure for what my dad did, and we are able to give the next generation a legacy of kindness, generosity, and strength to build their own lives upon. God is doing what He promised in Exodus 20:6 (NLT): "I lavish unfailing love for a thousand generations on those who love me and obey my commands."

The Bible says, "Let us not grow weary while doing good, for in due season we shall reap if we do not lose heart" (Galatians 6:9). My dad didn't grow weary doing good, and we are still reaping all he sowed. Whether he realized it or not, through the little choices he made, day in and day out, a beautiful legacy was created. He, like that oak tree in our yard, became a planting for God's glory (see Isaiah 61:3). You may think the small things you do on a daily basis don't matter in the grand scheme of things, but they do. You're sowing what others may reap. Even if you don't live to see it grow tall, you're watering a tree that could offer shade to the next thousand generations.

Finding Beauty in the Mess

What kind of legacy do you want to leave?
How can you be intentional to sow and water those seeds?

LOOK HOW FAR YOU'VE COME

Elaine Fisher

Those who look to him for help will be radiant with joy; no shadow of shame will darken their faces.

Psalm 34:5 (NLT)

While my mom and I were working on this devotional, I had a moment that stopped me in my tracks. I was having brunch with a friend, and she started asking me about my testimony. I shared with her some of the stories you've read in here and others I rarely share publicly. We both marveled as we reflected on the secret life I had lived and how God met me right there in my mess.

Then she asked me a question I had never been asked before, "Do you still have any side effects from that season?"

I thought for a moment and responded, "Honestly, no." As I left brunch, I reflected on that question, and my eyes filled with tears. I thought to myself, *Look how far you've come.*

I remembered how I used to fear telling my story because it would cause me to replay the details of my past in my mind. It was like a reel on repeat. I used to hate going to sleep because every time I closed my eyes, I would be flooded with memories, words, and images. It was a constant battle for my mind. And while I still have to guard my thoughts, this specific area has gotten so much easier. Now, if a memory pops up, it doesn't carry the same weight of shame and pain as it once did.

As I started to reflect on what had changed, I knew it wasn't just because time had passed. "Time heals all wounds" is a myth the enemy wants us to believe so we don't deal with a wound and stay in bondage. And while sharing my story helped me formulate my words around what I had experienced, it didn't take away the pain. Honestly, healing is a much more involved process.

Have you ever thought about how God designed our bodies to have reactions to kickstart the healing process? For instance, when you get a cut, your body starts a four-step process. First is hemostasis, which activates your body's natural reaction to restrict blood flow to that area to stop the bleeding. The second stage is inflammation,

> **Take time to celebrate each step of the process, even if it's slow and messy and you're struggling to see the end.**

which prevents the spread of infection and sets the stage for the repair process. Third is proliferation, which focuses on filling, covering, and stabilizing the wound. Fourth is remodeling or resolution, and the core aim during this step is to grow strong and flexible new tissue. Most of us know the healing process isn't pretty—actually, sometimes it's kind of gross—and it often requires work, care, and time to achieve complete healing.

Why did I take you down this rabbit trail about how our bodies are designed? Because the same God who created your body to have a physical reaction to kickstart the healing process also created and designed you for emotional and spiritual healing processes too. Colossians 3:9-10 in the New Living Translation says, "For you have stripped off your old sinful nature and all its wicked deeds. Put on your new nature and *be renewed as you learn* to know your Creator and become like Him" (emphasis added). Notice the words, "be renewed as you learn." This shows that God designed us to experience a renewal, a healing process that helps us to become more like Him.

The reason I can stand here in awe and say, "Look how far I've come" is because I have turned to Jesus at every step of the way. I made the choice every day to keep showing up at His feet. Like washing out a cut daily and covering it with a bandage, you take care of emotional and spiritual wounds by showing up at Jesus' feet daily.

Proverbs 16:3 (NLT) says, "Commit your actions to the LORD, and your plans will succeed." That word "commit" in this verse means to roll away or remove. It describes a camel transporting a heavy load, but when the burden becomes too heavy for the camel, it kneels down, and everything it's carrying rolls off its back. This visual is the perfect picture of what our part is each and every day. We need to come to the feet of Jesus, kneel down, and let the load of life roll off our backs. All throughout the Bible, God tells us that if we will direct our attention to Him, He will take our burdens, lift us up, and take care of us. He alone is our Healer.

We have shared so many different stories throughout this book. You have heard of some of our highs, our lows, and our in-betweens. Friend, I want to encourage you, wherever you are today, if you are healing and growing, it's a good sign. In the middle of a process, we can sometimes feel like we should be further along—more in control, less triggered, more joyful, more healed. Maybe you think you should have lost more weight by this point or controlled your anger better or whatever your "better" is. But we want you to remember that you don't have to be at the end of your journey to look back and say, "Look how far I've come." Take time to celebrate *each step* of the process, even if it's slow and messy and you're struggling to see the end. Run to the feet of Jesus, and allow Him to wash and stitch up your wounds. Look to Him for help, and let Him do a mighty work that breaks off shame and allows you to be radiant with joy.

Finding Beauty in the Mess

Lay your burdens at Jesus' feet right now, and let Him continue to heal your heart. And don't forget to look back and celebrate how far you've come.

THANK YOU

To the love of my life, Robert. Thank you for supporting and encouraging me to share these stories. I loved you from the moment of our first kiss on my back porch, and it's only grown exponentially since then. I'm so thankful for you and all that God has done in our lives.

To all my kids: Josh and Hannah, James and Bridgette, Ethan and Elaine. It has been my absolute pleasure watching you grow up and serve the Lord. You are the greatest story I've ever been part of writing.

To my grandchildren. You light up every day of my life. Always remember your Gigi loves you with all her heart, no matter what, forever and always.

— Debbie

To my husband, Ethan. You are a gift from God that reminds me of His grace every day. Thank you for loving all of me and encouraging me to be who God has called me to be. You always bring out the best in me, and I am forever grateful.

To my children: Adde, Kate, Preston, and Jackson. Mom life really *is* the best life! You four are my answered prayers, and I am excited to watch y'all change the world. Thank you for your sacrifices as we do ministry as a family.

To my mom and dad. Thank you for your dedication to the Lord. You have plowed ground and planted seeds that we will all reap. Thank you for loving me, extending grace toward me, and helping me develop the gifts God has given me. I am honored to be your daughter, and I pray God continues to use our journey for His glory!

— Elaine

To Lawrence, thank you for bringing this idea to us. It wasn't as easy as you originally predicted, but it was so worth it!

To Katie and Stacy, thank you for the time you spent with us to hear our hearts and for using your gifting with words to bring our stories to life.

To Peyton, thank you for the beautifully eye-catching, fun, and *messy* cover design.

To Chasity, Leila, and the rest of the Gateway Publishing team who helped pull this book together, thank you!

We couldn't have done this book without you, and while you each served a part behind the scenes, your gifts are helping propel this message of hope and encouragement around the world.

— Debbie + Elaine

ABOUT THE AUTHORS

Debbie and her high school sweetheart, Robert, have been married for forty-three years. They have three adult kids—Josh (married to Hannah), James (married to Bridgette), and Elaine (married to Ethan)—and nine grandchildren. Her family is the best thing about her life! Robert and Debbie founded Gateway Church in Southlake, Texas, in 2000, which has since grown to more than 100,000 active members. Debbie led the women's ministry at Gateway for many years and is the visionary founder of Pink Impact, a Gateway women's conference. Her heart is to help women understand who they are in God so they can discover their destinies and experience victory in life. As a wife who witnessed God turn her marriage around, she delights in encouraging women to believe God can and will do the same for them. She currently serves as an executive pastor but takes every opportunity to live the grandmother life (they call her Gigi) when she can! She never thought she'd write a book with Elaine about their family and experiences, but God had other plans . . . and she's so glad He did!

Elaine and her husband, Ethan, have been married for thirteen years, and they have four kids: Adde (10), Kate (8), Preston (7), and Jackson (5). As a pastor's kid, Elaine always had an awareness of the Lord, but she didn't develop a personal relationship with Him until she hit rock bottom at nineteen years old. Ever since, she has been passionate about helping people by sharing authentic revelation from the lessons she is learning along the way as God writes her story of redemption and freedom. In 2019, she and Ethan moved to Houston, Texas, to plant Gateway Church Houston, where she is on the executive team and serves as a teaching pastor. Elaine is an engaging communicator and has been a sought-after speaker at churches, conferences, and on television. Elaine sees it as a great honor to write a book with her best friend, and she is so grateful that her mom didn't give up on her in the early days because today their friendship is such a gift.

We'd love to hear
your feedback!

Leave a review on Amazon.

Explore Other Resources
From Gateway Publishing

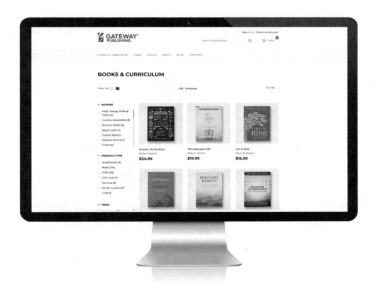

Visit GatewayPublishing.com

Gateway Publishing's purpose is to carry out the mission and vision of Gateway Church through print and digital resources to equip leaders, disciple believers, and advance God's kingdom.